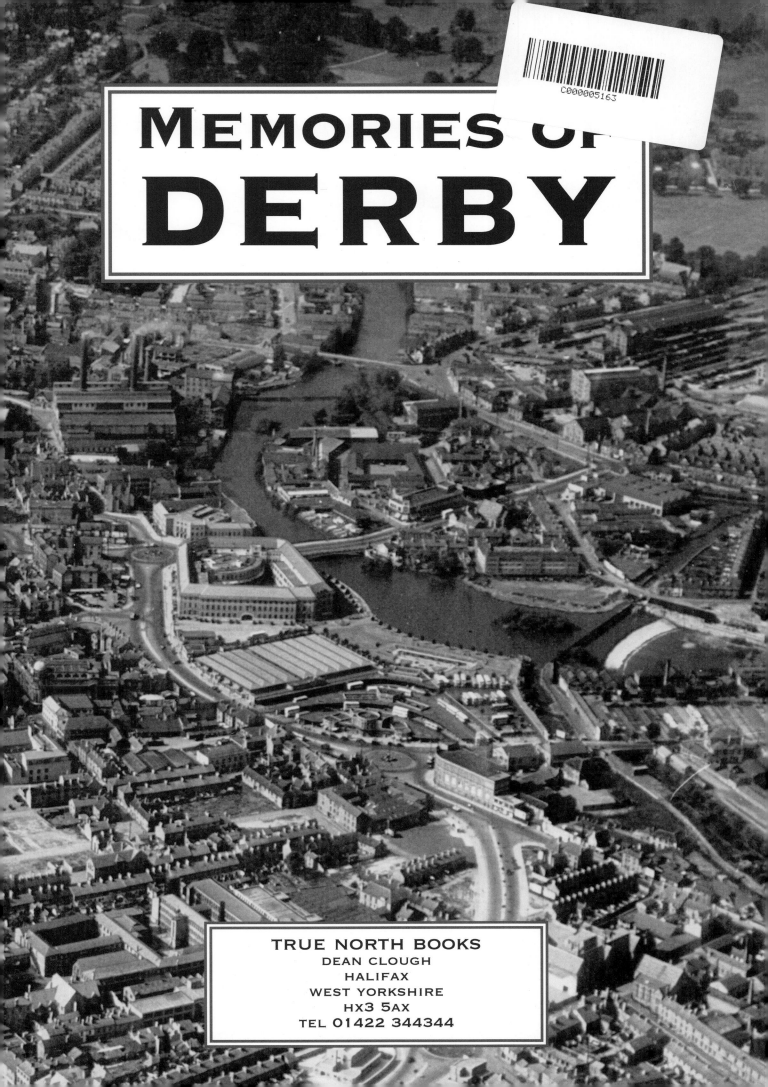

MEMORIES OF DERBY

TRUE NORTH BOOKS
DEAN CLOUGH
HALIFAX
WEST YORKSHIRE
HX3 5AX
TEL 01422 344344

THE PUBLISHERS WOULD LIKE TO THANK THE
FOLLOWING COMPANIES FOR SUPPORTING THE
PRODUCTION OF THIS BOOK

MAIN SPONSOR
RYKNELD TEAN LIMITED

ACRES (WILLINGTON) LIMITED

COE'S (DERBY) LIMITED

EGGLESTON BROS LIMITED

JAMES HARWOOD LIMITED

THE HORTICULTURAL & GENERAL STANDARD MANUFACTURING
COMPANY LIMITED

WJ PARRY & COMPANY (NOTTINGHAM) LIMITED

QUARNDON ELECTRONICS LIMITED

J SEAMER & SON LIMITED

SHEVILL PARKES & COMPANY LIMITED

JM TATLER & SON LIMITED

THORNTONS PLC

WALBROOK HOUSING ASSOCIATION LIMITED

G WALTHALL & SON LIMITED

WE WATTS LIMITED

WILLIAMS PLC

WW WINTER LIMITED

First published in Great Britain by True North Books
Dean Clough
Halifax HX3 5AX
1998

ISBN 1 900 463 37 7

Introduction

Welcome to *Memories of Derby*, a look back on some of the places, events and people in the city which have shaped the lives of local people over a period of around half a century. The following pages are brought to life by a selection of images from the not-too-distant past, chosen according to their ability to rekindle fond memories of days gone by and show how people used to shop, work and play in the area where they grew up. Modern image reproduction techniques have enabled us to present these pictures in a way rarely seen before, and the lively design and informative text has attempted to set the book apart from some of the other works available.

The chosen period is one which generally contains events within the memory of a large number of people in Derby - this is not a book about crinolines or bowler-hats! Neither is *Memories of Derby* a work of local history in the normal sense of the term. It has far more to do with entertainment than serious study, but we hope you will agree it is none the worse for that. It is hoped that the following pages will prompt readers' own memories of Derby from days gone by - and we are always delighted to hear from people who can add to the information contained in the captions so that we can enhance future editions of the book.

Many local companies and organisations have allowed us to study their archives and include their history - and fascinating reading it makes too. The present-day guardians of the firms concerned are proud of their products, the achievements of their people and the hard work of their forefathers whose efforts created these long established organisations in the first place. We are pleased to play our part by making it possible for them to share their history with a wider audience.

When we began compiling *Memories of Derby* several months ago we anticipated that the task would be a pleasurable one, but our expectations were greatly surpassed. There is a growing appetite for all things 'nostalgic' and we are pleased to have played a small part in swelling the number of images and associated information available to the growing number of enthusiasts.

There is much talk in modern times about the regeneration of the local economy, the influx of new industries and the challenge of attracting new enterprise from other regions to Derby. And quite right too. We could, however, make the mistake of thinking that the changes are all happening *now*, but the reality is that there have always been major developments going on in the city. 'Change' is relentless and the photographs on the pages in the book serve to remind us of some of them.

Memories of Derby has been a pleasure to compile. We sincerely hope you enjoy reading it.

Happy memories!

TEXT	BRYAN HUNT
COVER DESIGN/PHOTOGRAPH COMPILATION	MARK SMITH
DESIGNERS	MANDY WALKER, NICKY BRIGHTON AND CHRISTINE GALE
BUSINESS DEVELOPMENT EDITOR	ANDREW HALES

CONTENTS

Around the city centre

WW Winter Limited

Michael Thomas Bass was born in 1799, son of William Bass, the Burton brewer who established his brewery at Burton in 1777. His son Michael followed his father into the brewing business. Michael was MP for Derby for 35 years and his heart was set in the town. In 1867 he gave money to buy land to build a recreation ground on Siddals Road. It is still known as Bass' 'rec', and many have enjoyed fairs and the circus there. The open air swimming baths which Bass had built in 1873 in Derby town were almost as long lasting; free to the swimmers, they were still in use up to the 1940s.

In 1874 Michael Bass gave money towards the cost of a new public library of which the first stone was laid by Bass himself on October 25th 1876. This ceremony was followed by a procession and musical entertainments. The official opening was on June 28th 1879. Mr Bass

had received Royal treatment. The streets were decorated and bands played him in from the railway station to the library building, which as locals will know includes the museum and art gallery. The statue of Michael Bass was unveiled six months after he died at the age of 85. It was erected in the market place in October 1884 and is the work of the famous sculptor Sir Joseph Boehm. It was later repositioned in a former garden adjoining the museum.

In 1942 the statue was almost lost to the people of Derby when it was donated to the war effort to be melted down for recycling into war weapons. Fortunately it was rescued by a Councillor before ill could befall it. In 1964 the statue was moved a short distance, and again in 1993 to its present position in Museum Square.

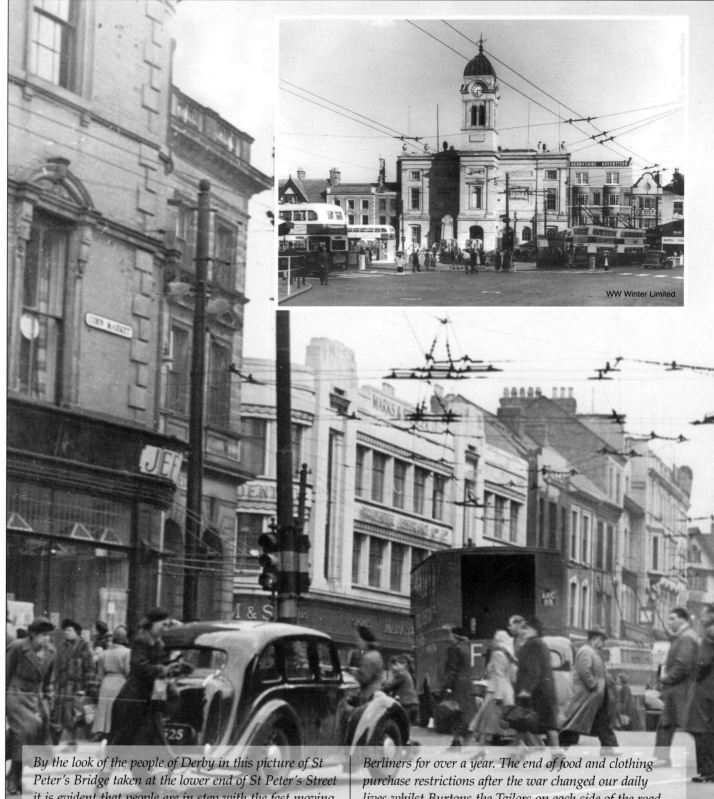

WW Winter Limited

By the look of the people of Derby in this picture of St Peter's Bridge taken at the lower end of St Peter's Street it is evident that people are in step with the fast moving times. Events in this year of 1948 outside the town would affect every one of these people, and everyone who has been to see the doctor, for this was the year Health Minister Aneurin Bevan announced the introduction of the National Health Service - and over 47 million Britons were treated in the first 12 months. Air freight transport rose to new heights with the Russians blockading Berlin, and we and the Americans broke the blockage by air lifting enough food to feed and warm the Berliners for over a year. The end of food and clothing purchase restrictions after the war changed our daily lives whilst Burtons the Tailors on each side of the road were changing the way we looked with non-utility clothing, and with all the changes came prosperity for the survivors: those who came back from the armed forces and those to whom they returned. All those who had contributed in one way or another to the victory had money to spend, and here they are, taking it out of the Midland Bank on the left by the traffic signals, and spending it on fine clothes, over the road at Marks and Spencers.

Inset left: This view of the Derby market place of the 1950, you are admiring the south side of the fourth Guildhall. To the right of it is the Derbyshire Advertiser office, a conversion from the handsome bow-fronted Cross Keys Inn with Frosts the butchers beyond.

The overhead trolley-bus power-lines tend to spoil the facade but a price had to be paid for progress in public transport.

Forty-three years earlier, the last horse drawn tram drew into the centre of Derby. Electric trams had already been running for three years, and went clattering and grinding their way round Derby until the mid 1930s. The trolley buses which replaced them were quick, clean, and, in today's language 'green'. Unfortunately few other towns and cities continued to invest in them, and after 30 years of excellent service new trolley buses were discontinued. Parts were hard to obtain, so maintenance of the Derby fleet was no longer an option, all overtaken, at last, by the march of time.

It's good to see that the war memorial is so prominent. At the time of the picture the road was open to two way traffic in either direction, but nowadays it is a pedestrianised zone. The clock was a gift to the town by the famous Derby clockmaker John Whitehurst and was subsequently reclaimed and gilded by John Smith. For many people it is perhaps the focal point of Derby city now as then when most events of importance seemed to be centred here.

Below: The Castle and Falcon in The Morledge, seen centre-picture, was afterwards demolished and rebuilt on the corner of East Street, which was formerly Bag Lane. On the left on the sky line is the ice factory of the Derby Cold Storage Company. The efficiency of this facility was inadvertently put to the test by the photographer who was commissioned to take some shots of the interior of the refrigeration plant. With his blood pumping well and his adrenaline high, he was eager to get on with taking photographs of the frozen fish and meat, although he was dressed for normal outdoor temperature.

'Will you be alright in there?' the manager asked. 'Right as a trivet,' answered Hubert, checking his camera, and went inside the store. He endured it for about three minutes, by which time he was chilled to the bone and his joints were stiffening. Fortunately, no long term harm was done, and he continues to take historic photographs, though not in 'freezers'.

WW Winter Limited

WW Winter Limited

Above: Here is a 1950s look at The Morledge, modernised according to the great Central Derby plan, and taken from Cockpit Hill which is named after the barbarous sport that took place there in olden times. For some time after the 'sport' was abolished a steel frame remained, fencing off the pit to serve as an historic curiosity.

The photograph is intended to show the spaciousness and modernity brought about by progress taking place in Derby centre at the time. By contrast, the pinnacled tower of All Saints rises on the left. The church was elevated to cathedral rank in 1977, so giving Derby the 'City' status. The smoke stacks behind the Council House disappeared with the destruction of the power station, which was built to ensure power to cater for all the city's growing needs, especially in the days of the trolleys buses.

Incidentally, the photographer is standing near the junction of Cockpit Hill with Siddalls Road, site of the first pot work in town and forerunner of Crown Derby.

Any book about Derby that doesn't mention 'Mad Harry' has missed one of the great characters of the time, for he was known as the fastest selling, quick auctioneer style stall holder in the market. The term 'mad' was affectionate, only used to describe his flamboyant style which could draw a crowd out of thin air and have them eager to buy his wares until they cleared his stock.

Above right: This intriguing view, taken where The Cornmarket meets St James Street in the 1930s poses as many questions as it answers, of people if

not of the place. Looking directly down towards Market Head, you have a clear view of Barlow Taylor and Company's building which, (as you will probably know if you have ever arranged a mortgage in Derby) became the Derbyshire Building Society. When the picture was taken the Old Wine Vaults pub, which disappeared in 1971, was next to Barlow Taylor, and beneath the concealing canopies at pavement level would be The Midlands Drapery store at the corner of St Peter's and East Streets.

In the foreground, on the left hand side, the policeman on point duty has his attention divided between looking at the photographer with his heavy professional camera on a tripod, and the flat-capped pedestrian wearing a heavy Crombie overcoat flapping open on a hot summers day. The policeman on traffic duty is fairly close to Barclays Bank, inside the St James building. Down the road on the right another watchful policeman has dismounted his bicycle so he can study the situation more closely, just like yourself.

This was the age of the 'New Look' in fashion when hemlines, which had been just above the knee to save material, took the country by storm and clothes rationing was finished. Could that be Charlie crossing the road to get a bottle of wine. That looks like Bert and Elsie heading for some butter and eggs from the Maypole. Fiona and Gareth hadn't even been thought of.

Some of the pedestrians in the picture could have been amongst the 8,000 Londoners who had come to Derby to escape the pilotless German V1/V2 flying bombs, and stayed after the war. Maybe you're even one of them, and remember those buzz bombs and the heart stopping times spent waiting from when you heard the motor stop, until it hit someone's home, leaving people helpless on the ground.

Nothing ever stands still. This 1948 picture shows H Samuels the jewellers, before it went on the move, taking its well known clock to the junction with Albert Street, and from Ramsdens restaurant it all changed in about 1968 for renovated and rebuilt premises such as Littlewoods store. Two years preceding the scene before your eyes, the Derby Rotary Club decided to promote foundation of a War Memorial Village for disabled servicemen at a cost of £100,000, with the project to be run by a co-operative of twenty four. The opening stages were celebrated when of June 27th 1949 the then Princess Elizabeth came and gave it the Royal seal of approval. By 1972 there were 38 homes, which later were absorbed into the community.

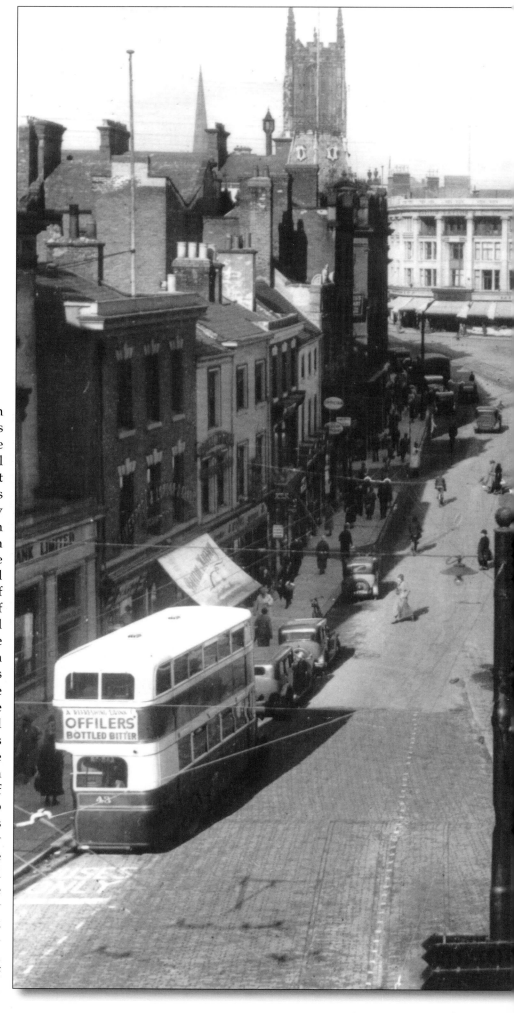

This delightful photograph features St. Peter's Street and is thought to date from the late 1930s. There is so much detail in the picture that an almost three-dimensional effect is created for the reader. Many well-known landmarks are in view and feelings of nostalgia are inevitably evoked by the combination of familiar old shops and bygone forms of transport. A spiders-web of overhead electric cables carried the power needed for the sturdy trolley buses which carried workers and shoppers from the centre of Derby to the suburbs. The clock outside H.Samuel's the successful and nationally-known jewellers was showing 12.30 p.m when the picture was taken and sun shades were out along much of the busy shopping street to protect stock and customers from the heat of the mid-day sun. These, remember, were the days before air-conditioned shops were commonplace. The picture affords a roof-top view across to the Guildhall clock tower on the right of the photograph and the dignified and equally imposing bell tower of Derby Cathedral on the left.

There is nothing more intriguing than having a place name in a town, and not having an explanation as to why it is so called, so maybe the reporter who first called this place The Spot in The Derby Weekly Mercury of the 1740s was just exciting the readers' curiosity. The Spot Rubber Company on the left had the business acumen to realise that naming itself after a part of Derby known to all could only enhance its reputation. This wide angle picture from just above The Spot at the end of St Peter's Street in the 1960s suggests it is an appropriate name, at any rate, for it looks like a good meeting place, "So just be there, on the Spot!"

The photograph is up-to-date enough for our younger readers, so if you were in the city before 1993 you'll remember the new clock-tower being built in the streets centre-spot, and if you are in your thirties you'll remember the changes on the right, which was cleared to make way for The Eagle Centre. The Green Dragon inn beneath the skyline sign Ind. Coop Burton Ales didn't see the 1970s out. It isn't the only brewery interest to have had its day on this site, where Ward's malthouse stood in the early 1740s. An earlier visit by royalty to Derby than that by Queen Elizabeth II and Prince Philip was commemorated on The Spot by the statue of Queen Victoria at the turn of century. You, or more likely your folks, might have seen their first moving pictures in The Kinema, opened here in 1910, a month after Florence Nightingale, the founder of nursing, died aged 90. Floral tributes at the memorial service for her at St Paul's Cathedral in London included those from Queen Alexandra the Queen Mother; a stunning cross of flowers from the London hospitals, flowers from the army in the shape of a lamp and more flowers still from those "who went into the valley of death, into the jaws of hell" - the remnants of the Light Brigade. The Kinema at The Spot had but another four years to wait before the first talking picture was heard there. Thomas Alva Edison, the American inventor, was still changing the lifestyle of Derby. First the gramophone. then the carbon microphone, then the incandescent light, and now talkies... what ever will he be up to next ? talking colour films?

Below: This familiar and much-photographed Derby street is well known to local folk. But the era featured is less familiar, for it reflects an age when it was less dangerous to loiter in the middle of a retail street among cars and buses which pose such a danger in modern times.

Thankfully the introduction of pedestrian precincts has added to the safety of town centre shoppers in shopping centres throughout the country.

The photographer was looking towards Market Head when he released the shutter for this picture. In the distance the distinctive light coloured outline of Barlow Taylor and Company's store can be seen. Of course, the building later found fame (and probably fortune) as the imposing public face of the Derby Building Society.

The tudor-styled property on the right of the street has always created interest in Derby. It was best remembered as the home of Cox and Malin and the location of their wine importing business which was to display the *Guinness is Good For You* sign for many decades. Cox and Malin's business stood between two other retail outfits which had achieved national importance. One was H. Samuel's, remembered in Derby as in other locations, for its distinctive exterior clock and reputation for supplying a wide range of good-quality, affordable items of jewellry.

It would be interesting to know just how many Derby couples have peered through Samuels' window, prior to making their commitment to each other with symbolic band of gold bought here.

Above: This photograph was taken from The Council House balcony, looking down Derwent Street onto the Market Place square. The most prominent building is the Guildhall, with its distinctive copper-domed clock-tower where lots of couples used to meet. On the left side street corner, by the zebra crossing, is Phillipsons store, which was the forerunner of the garden-centre establishments.

Beyond the bus picking up passengers at the bus shelter is the Market Place, which has long been a passenger ascending/descending point, from the days of two wheeled handsome cabs and four wheeled 'growlers'. Thrown the years the Market Place has seen horse drawn trams and buses, electric trams and trolleys, diesel and petrol buses. The Market Place is where cycling clubs would meet to set off for the day; likewise the Ramblers Association, and the trippers. It was also the assembly place for the floats in the processions going to Derby carnivals at Markeaton Park.

Above right: Because the Market Place has changed so much since the 1950s, this photograph will remind you of what it was like before in more detail. Most of this property, with the exception of Barlow, Taylor & Co, was demolished to make way for The New Assembly Rooms, and Barlow Taylor & Co moved in 1980. Their premises were taken by The Derbyshire Building Society.

Next door were the Old Wine Vaults, owned at the time of the photograph by Offilers. Before that it was Bowyers Vaults, and before that it was Brentnalls Wine Vaults. It was probably always known as 'The Sub', through which you entered. Next right to the Old Wine Vaults was Corbys, who were in the interior decorating trade.

In the offices next door D.S.Butler sold office furniture and was also in the printing business, whilst the shop at street level behind the parked sports car was Elliot's the Tailors and Outfitters, with a wholesale drapers' entrance right beside. The upper deck of the bus is bisecting a charity shop we take to belong to the Oxford Famine Relief enterprise 'Oxfam', above which is the Midland School of Motoring.

Below: On the right hand side of Albert Street, seen from its junction with Victoria Street, there is the former Trent bus station, with its panelled roof and triangular infill. Before it was a bus station it was a fish market, and after it was pulled down in 1986 it was used as a bus park, where on a cold and frosty morning at start up time you couldn't see across the road for exhaust smoke.

By the zebra crossing there used to be a cafe, which became a store, where we are told the bus fare-takings were deposited. On the left hand side of the road the vertical cafe sign was sufficient to those in the street at that time a guarantee of a good snack or full meal, backed as it was by the resources and reputation of the Co-op in Derby.

This panoramic view is of Derby as it stood on the brink of the Second World War, looking at the City Centre from the majesty of its cathedral tower. What draws the eye immediately is the light coloured building at centre picture which represents the handsomely copper topped dome of the Corn Exchange building which first shone golden in the sun on Albert Street in 1861.

Diagonally down right is the huge single span saddle-roof of the Indoor Market Hall. Continuing the line down right you can admire the magnificence of the Guildhall with its domed clock tower

rising over a hundred feet and dominating the entire foreground of the picture. Next to it on your right are the bow-fronted windows of the Derby newspaper offices. Returning to the Exchange building at centre, to your left is the Council House under construction. Before it, diagonally down left, is the Phillipson store and still on the same line is the old Assembly Rooms building. In all this we can find evidence of the hopes and aspirations of the builders of Derby. It's a jig-saw of many pieces about who dared and won their moment in the history of a great city.

Above: You are on Victoria Street, looking up Green Lane with Ranby's store now Debenham's on the right. At the other side is Woolworths, which opened its doors in 1911. In those days it was themed on the America five and ten cent store, and advertised that no single item cost more than sixpence. Next to Woolworths was Jeromes, the while-you-wait portrait photographers, in case you needed a passport picture for your trip on the Titanic, just launched down its Belfast slipway. On the corner with Green Lane was Meesons Ltd, and the area where the lorry and van are coming out of Green Lane has since been paved over.

Above right: The tower of the Church of All Saints, second highest in England after the Boston Stump, still dominates the scene from Corporation Street, taken from The Council House, looking straight down Full Street.

Now was the time of demolition. Our needs were changing, so the Assembly Rooms have been re-assembled (left). In 1967 the church of St Alkmunds was in the way of the proposed Inner Ring Road. The moving finger writes that where it stood is now a part of the new St Alkmunds Way. Derby power station, built in 1920, was closed in 1970. That's the police station on the right of the picture. The Derby Corporation vehicles parked in the foreground show the value of good planning.

This is Derby Market Place taken from the Guildhall in the 50s, as we can tell from the cars parked in the centre. The building on the far right is the Old Assembly Rooms which were built for social gatherings which gave the young people opportunity to enjoy dances and soirees, parties and performances in an easily chaperoned situation, as well as its prime purpose as a meeting place for polite society. The Old Assembly Rooms featured tea rooms on the ground floor. and a large ballroom on the first floor. It was a favourite venue for performances by the Derby Choral Society Post war it was renovated in 1948 and the roof was replaced six years later. The fire of 1963 provided good reason to build anew. The new Assembly Rooms are now behind the war memorial, as seen from this angle of the camera. Work started in '73 and the project was completed in time for a royal opening by Queen Elizabeth the Queen Mother on 9th November 1977, the year Derby achieved City status.

The cenotaph in the foreground typifies every village, town and city in the country which has its war memorial to those who died for Britain. The inscription here reads 'For Faith and Hope and Righteousness'.

Above: Midland Road in the late 1930, from near its junction with London Road. The Midland railway station stretches across the far end of the road. From the start of the railway era twelve years went by before Derby decided it was a viable alternative form of transport and invested. Mineral ores and coal interests were the prime movers, so to speak, in moving with the pressure of those competitive times. The coal mine owners had meetings which resulted in the formation of the North Midland Railway Company, and on May 30th 1839 the first train wheels rolled along the Midland Counties permanent way. Francis Thompson made hasty arrangements to construct a railway station, which was organised to accommodate the North Midland and Midland Counties lines as well as the Derby Birmingham connection. Each company put up its own workshops, destined to become the great locomotive works of the future. May 30th 1839 was the official opening day of the Derby to Nottingham line but it wasn't until June 4th that some 500 passengers boarded the four trains. First class cost four shillings, second class half-a-crown (eight to the pound). Things moved fast from then on, and it was only a year later that lines were laid to connect Derby with other major cities, with a bridge over the river Trent, and Derby had the true interpretation of 'main-lining'. The Midland Railway Co

had its HQ in Derby by 1844, the station was rebuilt along more modern lines, and kept on being up-dated as demand dictated. It suffered a couple of bomb hits in 1941. but the mess was quickly cleaned up and damage was minimal. It was business as usual in no time and the war effort rolled on. In 1985 the station was demolished, its purpose served. Its time had come.

Right: Nothing stands in the way of progress in Derby, as the perception of what is beautiful and what is practical is always being re-assessed by each generation. Even in The Wardwick, Derby's splendid Free Library, Museum and Art Gallery, bathed in brilliant sunshine of the 1955, emphasis falls on the extension of 1915, which is well matched to the main building. The extension replaced the curator's house. Beyond the library is the Mechanics' Institute, which is now a part of the Co-op bank, and beyond that is the General Post Office with the neighbouring Post Office Hotel, which has since changed identity two or three times and at the last count was the Pit and Truffle. One last word on this unlikely name: it improves it to discover that the 'truffle' in question isn't the sweet found in modern boxes of chocolates; but an edible tuber which is delicious to eat, grows in the sub-soil and was, and still is, sought after by trained dogs and pigs, especially on the Continent.

A bird's eye view of Derby which dates from the 1960s. A wealth of information is contained within the view and most of Derby's major central streets and notable public buildings are visible. Virtually in the centre of the photograph Derby Cathedral reaches skywards as it had done for centuries. The meandering course of the Derwent with at least four of her bridges in view makes a charming sight. Close to her banks the Council House building looks impressive, as does the adjacent market area and nearby new bus station. These relatively modern facilities were completed only around half a century ago but not all of them were to survive to the present day. Perhaps the most striking modern feature of this photograph is the inner relief road and its intermittent roundabouts. The County Council Highway Authority was responsible for the controversial new roadway.

Nobody could argue that a problem existed in Derby as in every other town of her size at the time, but when plans were announced for the solution many people winced at the scale of the proposed changes. The 1960s plan included changes to the make up of the centre of Derby's retail heart. A new Littlewoods store was built on the site of Devonshire House. A massive roundabout would be built on the site of the former Cattle Market and the Methodist Chapel on King Street pulled down. The scheme was perhaps the most ambitious Public Works project the Derby has seen this century. It was completed, if these things are ever completed, in the early 1970s.

Above: This group of around 20 young lads can be seen running along one of Derby's suburban streets. Little is known of the purpose of their run if, indeed, 'a purpose' was needed. In days gone-by there was a bigger emphasis on the 'physical side' of recreational activities, and for obvious reasons. Money was more scarce than it is today and groups of youngsters would work hard to make their own entertainment, relying on traditional games, public parks, swimming baths and voluntary organisations such as the Scouts and Guides. Going to church was more common than it is today and church social activities and youth clubs had more influence on youngsters than is the case today. Often people would meet their future wives and husbands through church organisations - not that this is unheard of today of course, but in the era featured here it was certainly more common. All our lives have changed over the years and for the most part the changes have been for the better. As more houses began to benefit from central heating the effect was to make them seem bigger. Families need no longer huddle around one fireplace in order to keep warm, and when children began to have televisions and personal computers in their bedrooms the family unit was split forever. No wonder then that children no longer see being 'sent to their room' as the punishment we once did.

Left: If this photograph had been taken of the children's paddling pool in the Rykneld recreation ground a bit later on in the 1950s there would have been just the water, for the poliomyelitis scare came to these parts then and had people queueing up at doctors' surgeries for their anti-polio jabs.

The belief that the virus might be in the water broke the habit parents had of letting their children play in the park pool, together with the swings and roundabouts, sand pit, maypole and the like on sunnier days like this. So Derby has adjusted to changing times as always and redevelopment for this area is now the key.

WW Winter Limited

Above: "Oh, come listen to the band; oh the music's simply grand..." and so it was on this evening when there was a fine programme played for hundreds of brass band lovers in the Arboretum, the wonderland botanical gardens given to the town by Joseph Strutt for the lasting pleasure of its citizens. Joseph was evidently a fine man, both in mind and stature, concerned with the future recreational activities of Derby and its visitors. He was a man of vision with the where-withal to fund it, and in mid September 1840 thousands of Derby people flocked into the park to sing and dance and listen to the band. Later on the Arboretum was enlarged and 17 years after a spell as Prime Minister Lord Palmerston presented Derby with a pair of cannons - souvenirs from the Russian conflict. These were sited at the Arboretum, bringing echoes of the 1812 overture. He became Prime Minister again in 1859 until he died six years later, always a good friend of Derby.

'We cannot', as someone wisely said, 'turn back the clock.' What we can do is record the glorious past, turn on the light of remembrance of leisurely days and leafy ways in the heart of the city, close the eyes and open the ears to 'The Entry of the Gladiators', imagine the happy couples again dancing to 'The Emperor Waltz', and turn 'The Blue Danube' into the Blue Derwent.

Above right: The Centre of Education Ltd (CEL) who housed in St Peter's Church Yard on two floors in 1938. Prior to that it was round the corner down at the bottom of St Peter's Street. One amazing feature at the CEL was that its windows fooled your eyes into

WW Winter Limited

believing it had no glass in it. The glass was bowed, and the black foreground cast no reflections up. Despite this, simple and eye-catching trick, CEL disappeared in the early 1970s. Books cost from 1/6d in "real money," or seven and a half new pence in today's coinage. Penguin (paperback) books were always good value for money, though why they called themselves Penguin Books baffles me, unless the head office was in Antarctica. These were the days when everyone read books, and you might well have learned to read by studying Comic Cuts, The Wizard, the Adventure, the Magnet, What Katie Did and Girls' Own.

In the 1500s 13 poor folk and their families were housed in the parish by the Trust set up by Derby dyer Robert Liversage. This was added to and wisely administered, building on success to become an inheritance for the City 400 years later on.

WW Winter Limited

Above: Derby's Grand Theatre, which stood in Babington Lane, was the brain child of Andrew Melville, the Birmingham manager and man of many parts.

It was in 1885 when he visited Derby and, naturally looking for a theatre, didn't find one. The theatre that had existed in Derby had lost its license in 1862 so; here was opportunity knocking for the visitor. Construction work began six months after his visit and the Theatre opened on Thursday March 25th 1886, and on Thursday May 7th 1886 it was the scene of a real tragedy, for it was gutted by fire which started as the actors were putting on their make-up for the evening performance. The event drew an audience of 20,000 to watch as everything went up except the frontage.

Melville was dressed to play the title role in his adaptation of the musical 'Rip van Winkle'. Unhappily two men were trapped perished. Andrew Melville died 10 years later.

The next 'Grand' opening was on Saturday November 13th 1886, attended by Thomas Roe MP and the Mayor Samuel Whitaker. This was an opera performed by the English Opera Company.

Amongst the star performers to play at the Grand was Lancashire's Gracie Fields in 1938, in a charity concert. Other famous names of the day included Ted Rae the comedian, Albert Tatlock of Coronation Street fame, Robertson Hare, Jack Howarth, Ronnie Ronald, Dicky Henderson, Morecambe and Wise, Arthur Lucan as Old Mother Riley, Donald Peers, Izzy Bonn, Frank Randall and lots more top performers. The Grand was the theatre of the people, and its shows had something for everyone.

Above: This comparatively recent view of the Morledge Market reveals the change that has taken place, from the times when everyone wore a hat to go out in, to recent time when only six per cent do, (not counting the policeman). What is important now is the emphasis on road safety in Derby, with a bobby on traffic duty at a zebra crossing, whilst on the notice-board on the right, the Derby Borough Road Safety Committee is keeping a tally of the casualty figures on the roads. By the number of people crossing the road towards you it is almost as though the crossing is somewhat askew for pedestrians carrying heavy shopping bags.

Right: Alveston is like the West side of Derby, since it was once the West side of Northworthy, before the Vikings came. Looking at the lake in Boden's Pleasaunce, as the 30 acres of recreation ground just off the London Road was once called, it's hard to believe there was once a spy running round without a stitch of clothing on. The wonder of words is that you can jump back in time just by starting a sentence, but this tale is told of a man who was trying to avoid a death sentence.

Handsome Prince Charles Edward Stuart, sometimes called The Young Pretender, had come down to Derby with his army of Scottish Highlanders, to parley with the Mayor and his councillors about support for his seizing the throne. Since the Mayor had been kicked down the stairs at Exeter House just previously things weren't going too well for the Prince.

Eliezer Birch was a spy for the establishment, when the Jacobite army caught him and locked him up in Exeter House, but on the cold and frosty morning of December 5th when the Prince was moving off towards Culloden, Eleizer forced the window casement of the room he was in, dropped to the ground two score feet below, scaled the garden wall, stripped off and dived into the freezing Derwent Navigation canal.

Better than hanging about, he thought; must keep the circulation going. He swam until exhausted, then legged it alongside the stream three miles to Alvaston, where an astounded Mistress Ridgeley took pity on him. After she recovered from her surprise, she helped him escape on horseback. That happened in 1745, just 194 years before the next bit of excitement hit Alveston, when the sirens sounded the alarm the day after Chamberlain declared war against Germany, giving the boys and girls in the army operating the ack-ack (anti-aircraft) guns at Alvaston Camp a chance to test their training. Nothing happened that time. Glad to say there was more action going on at the Rec cinema most of the war in Derby.

Below right: Saturday April 27th 1946 and what a triumph by The 'Rams', the Derby County soccer team which won the Football Association Cup Final against Charlton Athletic at Wembley stadium. The entire town was gripped with football fever in the days when many of the players were home grown. The score of 4-1 at the end of the game left no doubt about the Derby side's supremacy, having kicked the ball so hard it burst twice in succession playing against Charlton.

When skipper Jack Nicholas raised the cup on high the cheers rolled round the ground and went on whilst Jim Bullions, Horatio (Raich) Carter, Peter Doherty, Douglas (Dally) Duncan, Reg Harrison, Jack Howe, Leon Leuty, Walter Irvine, (Chick) Musson, Jack (The Old Warhorse) Stamps, and Vick Woodley went up to collect their cup-winners medals.

They came home to a welcome fit for heroes from the town, with a procession starting from the Baseball Ground and on round the town in an open top bus to a civic reception hosted by the Mayor on the police station balcony.

Everyone wanted to have a part of the action, not least the Parks and Gardens Department which put on this striking emblematic flower display in the Normanton Recreation Park.

Below: Once upon a time there was a well intentioned knight called Sir Francis Ley, who happened to have a foundry in Derby. He went to America and came back to Derby determined to found a baseball league, which he did.

The area beside the foundry was called the Vulcan ground, and when the baseball league waned because Derby won nearly all the time against the three other teams, it converted to the Derby County Football ground in 1895, but is still known to this day as The Baseball Ground.

Three times runners-up for the cup at the turn of the century, now look at the same breed of Derby County players, directors and officials 43 years later in 1946 with the FA Cup under their belt. 'The Rams', who may have their nickname from the mascot of the Sherwood Foresters, went on to win the Football League twice in the 1970s.

Our photograph shows the First team squad and directors in 1946 These are the men who made the never to be forgotten game possible: standing l to r: J Parr, J Bullions, J Nicholas (captain), V Woodley, J Howe, L Leuty, W Musson, Centre row: S Crooks, J Stamps, S Mcmillan (Manager), TE Wassell MBE (Vice Chairman of Directors), B Robshaw (Chairman of Directors), H Walker (Director), JR Cholerton (Director), P Doherty, R Carter, D Willis (Trainer), Front row: R Harrison and D Duncan.

WW Winter Limited

WW Winter Limited

Events and occasions

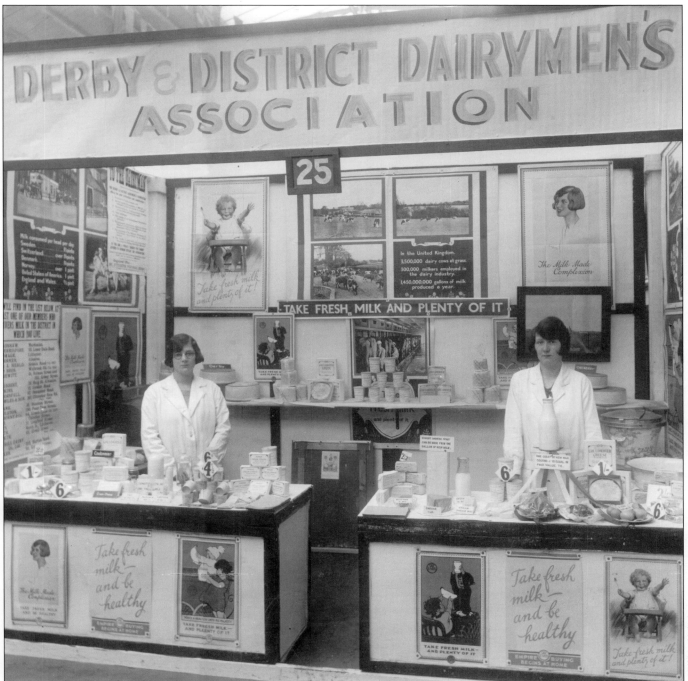

WW Winter Limited

Above: More than 40 members of the Derby and District Dairymen's Association subscribed to this exhibition stand in 1935, intent on making the public aware that milk, cheese and dairy products were as health giving as ever, good for building strong bones and teeth.

By this time Louis Pasteur's 'pasteurisation process' of raising the milk temperature to 145-150 degrees centigrade for half of an hour was in common practice before bottling. The roundsman's joke of passing a bottle across his face in response to the housewives' question 'Is it Pasteurised?' with the answer 'Well, if it wasn't before, it is now!' wasn't always appreciated.

Many milkmen in those days came by horse drawn cart, with churns of milk to measure out into your enamelled jug left on your step by long handled gill, pint and quarter gallon ladles, being careful to put your saucer back on the jug when he had finished. If you were at home, if your clock didn't keep good time you would know the right time once a day at least when the horse pulling the milk-cart would stop on the dot outside your house, come rain, hail or shine.

WW Winter Limited

WW Winter Limited

Above: *The Food Advice Bureau* was a wartime phenomenon. During the Second World War Britain was operating under a siege economy. Maintaining adequate supplies of food on the *home front* was one of the most challenging aspects of the war. Parks and gardens were ploughed up and planted with vegetables and other crops capable of adding to the nations food resources. The Womens' Land Army, an experiment tried during the First War, was established to boost the production of food and help replace some of the male agricultural labour force which had been called away to the front. Part of the solution was to grow more food, but another way of easing the problem was to educate housewives in ways of making otherwise unattractive foodstuffs fit for the dinner table. There was a war on waste and a campaign to make the best of what was available - from powdered egg and milk to all kinds of root vegetables and obscure cuts of meat. The situation in Britain contrasted sharply with conditions in Germany where rations were relatively generous and women were never completely mobilised to help the war effort.

Right: Taken in the Derby Carriage and Wagon Works Club of 1958 you can see over 200 young people respectfully listening in silence whilst the Lady Mayor Coun. Mrs Florence Riggott talks to them and wishes them a Happy Christmas from Herself and the Corporation. You were a credit to your parents if you were one of them, even if your folks didn't understand the new jazz jargon, because they could never be 'hip'. The party wasn't exactly 'groovy', and wrinklies were never going to 'dig-it man'. Contrast that with well mannered pair caught standing as The Mayor started speaking. They've come to a respectful stop and they are never going to become 'junkies'. That's not say say they never got the 'rock-and-roll' dance fever from America. did you? The Club was well known and patronised for a long time afterwards until it burnt down.

WW Winter Limited

Above: Those readers who have owned miniature electric train sets (and there were a lot sold in Derby), will remember the problems of using electric to stimulate steam trains. Not the lack of smoke and steam particularly, but the way steam trains pulled out of the station slowly, like a weight lifter building power from his lungs with oxygen before lifting, heaving a massive bar-bell weight overhead.

Then the steam locomotive would shudder with pleasure, wheel-spin into sync with line-grip, and the rhythm over the rail expansion joints would set up a satisfying, constant clickety click.

Not so the trolley, which, like your model electric train, had sufficient power to turn the wheels according to load carried, and immediate tyre grip on the road, giving truly remarkable acceleration.

The trolley-bus model pictured is a No 140 Guy BTX Trolley bus of 1934 vintage, in the Municipal Corporation Act Centenary Exhibition of 1935 in the Newlands St Drill Hall. It was a working model, powered, as were the full-size trolleys, by overhead cables. It was a tremendous attraction and never suffered from overtaking other trolley problems or the need to reverse.

Right: Derby Gas Light & Coke Company built in Friargate in 1889, seen here in the year 1953 dressed up for the Coronation. It used to be part of the East Midlands Gasboard showrooms, and nearby was St Werburghs church. The building is now a night club.

Princess Elizabeth, in the finest tradition of our monarchy, came to Derby on Monday 27 June 1949 to perform the official opening of The Council House (inset), a title it well justifies, with the smack of wisdom, and our long and honourable traditions invested for the beginning of a new era. The Princess would know that the Council House project had only just been finished in time for the military to requisition it for the duration of the war, and that it had only been handed back a few months before its royal opening. If the Mayor and Mayoress, Alderman Charles Frederick Bowmer and his wife, were slightly flushed it had nothing to do with the pandemonium which had been going on to get the reception area ready in time.

With the Princess came the Duke of Edinburgh and together they were made welcome with the full panoply of Derby's ceremonial figures and by its loyal subjects to the Crown. The royal couple came to enjoy the full splendour of the purpose built building, an ornamental pond in its precinct which featured bronze turtles, whilst the boy and goose statue from the Market Place now graced the frontage. The turtles afterwards decamped to Allestree Hall, and the boy and goose were to find a home in a corner of the City centre.

Whilst in Derby the regal pair made the most of their time. The Princess visited the Royal Crown Derby works where she was presented with replicas in porcelain of the famous Derby Dwarfs. The Duke of Edinburgh meanwhile went to see how the Rolls Royce Company was doing. The next time the the royal couple came to Derby was in 1977, to upraise Derby to the status of City. The entire County joined in the celebrations, and after dining with the Duke and Duchess of Devonshire the couple were driven from Chatsworth to Belper, famous for its association with Jedediah Strutt, the inventor, who had a cotton mill there in in the mid 1770s.

Next Their Royal Highnesses went on to The Matlocks, Bridge, Bath and Bank unified in 1927, there to see some of the most beautiful scenery in Derbyshire including the Heights of Abraham and High Tor. Finally they arrived at Chellaston's Darley Park Mansion where they were welcomed by the Mayor and Mayoress Alderman and Mrs Charles Bowmer and all the Corporation officers in full regalia, with a guard of honour of halberdiers, men-at-arms who by custom carried the combined spear-and-battleaxe halberds.

The wonderful day ended on a solemn note as the future Queen Elizabeth II dedicated the foundation stone of the war memorial to absent heroes.

Above: Just look at this Trades Fair display in the 1935 Newland Street Drill Hall. What a transformation took place to Derby City in the late 1920s after the huge power cable was floated down the Derwent and connection with the national power grid was made. Street gas lighting rapidly became a obsolete, older houses had their gas pipes sealed off and pavements were dug up to network the streets with the safe new power.

Safe, that is, if you didn't meddle with the unused bakerlite 2-pin plug mounted on the multi-pin socket by which you ran the wireless, the cylinder vacuum cleaner, one of the radiators like you can see in this photograph, and every electrical gadget as it came onto the market. Overload demand on the socket, spill water on it, put a lamp bulb in without switching off, the safety factors became important each time the newspaper reported an injury or fire. The plus side far outweighed the risks, especially as appliance of science made electricity safer with fuses, right up to circuit breakers for hedge trimmers and mowing machines in case you cut the cable in two.

Did you buy a two-bar, three-bar, even a four-bar electric fire? And did you go on holiday and wonder all week if you had switched it off in the back bedroom. How quickly it all happened, and the trolley buses which gave Derby pedestrians mobility from 1932 on disappeared, joining the long list of good intentions which just didn't make it. Not even the Derby power station remains, as the 'juice' now comes from the National Grid.

WW Winter Limited

WW Winter Limited

Above: The Kenning Motor Group's dynamics of 1938 is clearly seen on this 1938 display in Company premises, then on Queen Street. It made the point that Kennings meant reliability, and offered an after-sales service of vehicle inspection and repair which would keep the wheels turning, even extending to overnight repairs if necessary.

From George Kenning selling paraffin on the open market at Bakewell and offering home delivery we're told to becoming a nationwide vehicle hire business says much about the founder's drive to success, with a knighthood en-route.

A quirky report from chauffeur and handyman to Lady Kenning in her later years, John Bowler said he used to do the flower beds and cut the lawn and take her up the A6 to Darley Abbey post office to draw her pension in the early 1960s, when she was a widow in her 90s.

Top: In the never ending competition for sales, new products have to fight their way into the newspapers and magazines to gain your attention, in a persuasion process that never stops. One way the advertising agencies go about this is to announce the launch of a new product, for example, a 'Qualcast' light/weight electric grass cutting machine. 'Let's do it at a cocktail party attended by top executives like the Group Chairman (of the day), Mr Jobson and A.N. Other, to welcome a celebrity who has a business charisma and who has appeal for the potential customers. 'You know Noelle Gordon who plays a director in the television programme with the Birmingham Motel story-line 'Crossroads'! She would be perfect for this promotion. Ask our account executive to discuss it with the Qualcast advertising manager and see if it gells.' Even in those progressive days they might have been surprised at her smoking, for it was usually the men who enjoyed the macho image, but Noelle had the charm and confidence, and the professional nous to smile at the camera.

From apron strings to red tape

Rykneld Tean Ltd is part of Autoliv Inc and was formed by a merger in 1990 of two companies, Rykneld Mills Limited, a well established company in narrow fabrics and New Tean Hall Mills Limited which had been producing narrow fabrics at its Tean factory in Staffordshire for 250 years.

Rykneld Mills Ltd

It was around 1860 that the firm of J & C Lilley was founded for the manufacture of tapes, mostly for domestic purposes at that time. The Lilleys were a big family and in 1926 two grandsons of the founder set up Rykneld Mills Ltd. They spent some months erecting machinery, mostly carried out with the help of overtime workers in the evenings. They managed to get eight or nine looms ready for an official start on New Year's Day 1927.

Claude Lilley and his brother Leslie spent most of that first morning speculating as to what the future might hold, having burnt their boats by parting company with the family firm of J Lilley & Sons. Their object had been to make a place for their two younger brothers, Garford and Jack and they too became involved in a new company, Garford Lilley & Brother and ultimately the old firm was voluntarily liquidated.

From the production of tape for binding the edges of material and so-called 'red tape', which is really pink, Rykneld found ever-increasing applications for their product. They began to supply narrow woven fabrics to the electrical industry, the clothing, boot and shoe, carpets and furnishing, corset and hosiery trades, to name but a few. Soon they were producing them on an enormous scale.

Every modern aid was employed as it became available. This included a new service, the Business Reply Telegram, offered to customers free of charge for urgent orders. It worked by a complicated code of letters representing the degree of urgency, type of goods required, method of despatch and so on to save on Post Office charges.

Rykneld was incorporated under the Companies' Act in

1929, with 750,000 ordinary shares of 1s each offered at 5s 3d per share

A difficult period for the Company arose at the outbreak of the Second World War. A crisis arose when the management was required to turn over the production to the making of aircraft tapes and tapes for electric motors for submarines. Just as they were well started on this project, an official arrived to say that it was now the firm belief of the War Cabinet that gas would be extensively used and that Britain faced imminent defeat unless gigantic quantities of tapes for gas masks and anti-gas clothing were forthcoming without delay. An Admiralty representative stipulated the large quantities the firm was expected to supply but the difficulty was in obtaining the necessary quantities of yarn which was already becoming scarce.

With ingenuity and improvisation the yarn was obtained, but then came difficulties over labour. A vast number of the Mill's unmarried female staff had been switched to munitions production so that Rykneld was deprived of many of its highly skilled and productive operatives. The Company fell back on the services of married women who had previously worked for them. In this way the Mill succeeded in contributing a major proportion of the

Government's requirements in the hour of need. Two generations of 'know-how' on the part of the directors enabled the firm to make this rapid adaptation. Government Departments and electricity undertakings were among their thousands of active customers at home and abroad. The Mill began to supply the bedding industry with mattress tapes and divan pipings.

The electricity industry began to take about half of the total output, mostly for the insulation of dynamos, motors and cables, and for use in the manufacture of electrical generating and distribution plant for electrical undertakings. This was in addition to domestic requirements.

The production of Rykneld Mills was so varied that, although classified under the heading 'Textiles', a considerable proportion of its goods are supplied for industrial purposes. Consequently the Company was not susceptible to the recurring trade depressions which began to affect the textile industry.

Above: One of the making up lines in the 1950s.
Facing page, top: An early advertisement for a new company ordering service.
Facing page, bottom: An early winding machine.

Exports too were increasing, particularly to Australia, Canada and South America. Exports consisted of a whole product range from Rykneld. However, by virtue of Rykneld tape featuring in so much electrical and other equipment and in so many types of manufactured goods made in Britain for export, Rykneld 'intangible' exports assumed huge proportions.

By the end of the eighties 250 looms were weaving two and a half million metres of tapes and webbings per week which they supplied to customers including the Ministry of Defence, Silentnight, Pirelli and the Electricity Boards. The applications ranged from soldiers' packs to the tapes on ballet dancers' shoes.

The actual mill had become a

Rykneld is proud of its long tradition, and in the last fifteen years the Company has grown with the acquisition of six local smaller narrow fabric manufacturers, and the addition of braided and knitted cords to its range.

Rykneld is now at the forefront of rigid narrow fabric manufacture in the UK. Accredited with the international quality standard ISO 9002 since the early nineties the Company currently employs 170 people on four sites in Derby, Tean, Wirksworth and Milford. With a growing order book both in the UK and in Europe, and further afield, the Company is set to meet the challenges of the new millennium.

*Above: One of the weaving sheds at Rykneld Mill in the late 1930s. **Left:** An early warping machine. **Facing page, top:** An early calendering and glazing machine. **Facing page, bottom:** An early sizing machine. **Below:** Part of the Mill as it is today.*

listed building with a traditional outward appearance. The inside was a different story. All the old multi-shuttle looms have been replaced by modern high speed needle looms.

Today these looms are producing tapes and webbings made from all types of yarns, ie. cotton, polyester, nylon, glass, polypropylene etc. In addition, all types of special finishes can be applied to these products, to make them rot proof, water repellent, flame retardant and the company also owns its own Dyeworks at Milford.

In 1969 Rykneld was absorbed into the Marling Industries Group and subsequently, in 1998 into the Autoliv Inc, a Swedish based company whose main business encompasses automotive restraint systems like seatbelts and airbags.

Below right: Two distinctive columns frame the right hand edge of this photograph with elegant stone steps leading to the broad pavement below. Derby's imposing Council House building was opened by the popular Princess Elizabeth and her dashing husband, the Duke of Edinburgh, in 1949. Building work had started on the ambitious building project as far back as 1938, but, like so many non-essential projects of a similar nature, it was interrupted by the outbreak of the Second World War. During the conflict, in March 1942, the property, in its partially-completed state, was requisitioned by the RAF and used for a variety of wartime functions. Construction work was completed soon after the war ended and in 1948 and the whole of Derby felt honoured when the news came that Princess Elizabeth had agreed to visit the area to open the building. A rapturous welcome greeted the royal couple and it seemed as if the whole of Derby was decked out with flags and bunting. Cheering crowds lined the route taken by the gleaming black limousines and the loyal subjects of Derby cheered with delight as the couple appeared on the balcony of the newly-built Council House.

Bottom: This magnificent iron railway bridge was constructed in

1877 in the Friar Gate area of Derby and named after the owner of Handyside's iron foundry, which was located along Duke Street. The railway age came to Derby in 1839 with the opening of the Midland Counties Railway's line. The first railway service linked Derby with Nottingham a journey which took just over forty minutes in those early days of stream transportation. The Great Northern Railway arrived in Derby in the 1870s and soon made a considerable impact on the landscape of the town as well as greatly enhancing the services available to the travelling public.

On the move

How often have you seen a Derby Corporation bus broken down? It's a very rare occurrence, and the reason is the policy of buying the best for the fleet from the outset, and with a strict overhaul and maintenance routine, the service is always tip-top. The depot was actually built for the R.A.F. at the beginning of the war, for hiding things.

The skilled team which keeps these buses on schedule is proud of its fine record and the Derby Bus Corporation garage docking bays in the Ascot Drive Depot are as well-kept as the vehicles themselves. Neither is the significance of the Depot's location lost the teams and bus crews. For Derby, Ascot and going places by horsepower have been synonymous since the 12th Earl of Derby had the notion to start a race for three year old race horses.

The origins of the name "Typhoo' may be in danger of being forgotten though, which would be a pity, seeing we drink so much of it. Under calm conditions in the China seas between July and November the heat from the sun sometimes causes a cyclonic disturbance which fortunately reaches our shores as a modest sea breeze which like the tea you no doubt find refreshing.

WW Winter Limited

Above and right: As far back as the the early 1690s, Derby business men had been hankering after water borne transport for the basic industries. George Sorocold finally came up with a plan in 1703 for a Derby canal as an extension of the Trent and Mersey Canal, reaching the town by locks, and rising to provide access to the main industries before wending its way through watermeadows over eight miles eastward to the Erewash canal. All this was completed by 1796. Road transport was horse drawn in those days, not yet seen as a real competitor to the canal, but in 1735 Nottingham, Derby and London were connected by stage coach which ran a regular service to the George in Irongate. Turnpike tolls were introduced a few years later so that by the early 1800s new roads were being built, old roads improved and coach travel was networking a wide area around Derby.

The invention of the internal combustion petrol driven engine in 1884 changed everything and, saving the days of the trolley, enabled the advance of the town to the magnificent practicality of Derby's purpose built bus station. This reshaped the town centre round Cockpit Hill and the Morledge with modern elegance, its curved platforms making the most of the restricted area by 1932. A most successful part of the Derby Central Improvement Scheme was completed.

From then on the bus station became the exchange centre for passengers who wanted to get to any part of Derbyshire by road and many a one going to see friends and relatives from the outskirts would know to bestir themselves when they saw Harts the Chemists shop on the precinct through the bus window. The chemist shop was the most visible of several on the parade and other facilities there included a Ladies Waiting Room, built where the mortuary used to be. For the inner city traveller what was thought to be the final connection was made in 1973, with the bridge giving access to The Eagle Centre. The bridge has since been demolished.

WW Winter Limited

Above: Looking at the picture taken of The Morledge from Cockpit Hill in 1936 you see a Derby in the midst of change, with evolution moved into top gear by a new progressive need to do things, go places and see things. There is the timeless backdrop of All Saints Church (a cathedral from 1927). To its right is St Alkmunds with its fine spire and St Mary's just behind it. Moving forwards in time, in the centre left of the picture you see the chimneys overtopping the generating plant of Derby's electrical power station, built in the 1920s and demolished in the 1970s.

Nearer still to present day, the trolley bus presence is a growing sign of Derby's modernity, but single decker buses have already appeared, (from memory) in a cream and green livery. From the photograph, what is the biggest contrast in transportation, would you say? The motorbike and side-car combination against the milk-float, or what about the same milk float just about to pass the char-a-banc coming in the opposite direction ? Did you ever go on a works trip in the old style 'Sharrarbang' to Alton Towers, or come home from Tutbury with a piece of cut crystal glass after watching the Horn Dance at Abbots Bromley (first Monday after September 4th)? Did your husband take you shopping in town on Saturdays in the sidecar? Maybe you moved a bit further away from the next street to the factory with your new mobility!

The Johnny on the Corner' in the Panama hat was a familiar sight in 1936, scratching a living in hard times for some. He wasn't interested in the liner 'Queen Mary' taking the rich and famous on the Atlantic run to America; more likely he was disturbed to learn, as he stood there on this day, that there was a place called Jarrow full of unemployed shipbuilding workers who were marching the 291 miles to London and might as well have stayed at home.

Below: We have come into the garage section of the Derby Corporation's Ascot Drive Bus and Trolleybus depot, next to the repair section which always kept the trolley buses at full strength.

The last trolley to run in Derby departed on its final run on Sept 9th 1967: a rare occasion on which it was late coming back - it left the city centre at 11.00am and didn't come back until the next day.

The driver and his conductor decided that after covering the usual route. they would do all the other routes in Derby as well; and if they had-a ticking-off from the inspector when it finally pulled in, it was worth it for they also got a lot of smiles as well.

Right: The successor to the electric tramcar was first called a trackless tram. The trolley buses, as they quickly became known, were made very welcome in Derby as they were so quick, clean and comfortable. The first trolley bus route in the 1930s went along Nottingham Road as far as the cemetery, made possible after the Ministry of Transport inspector checked out the fledgling system and permission was then given for a trolley-bus service to the new terminus at The Creamery in Chaddesden.

That was on January 4th 1932, and five days later the Mayor of Derby, Alderman William Henry Salisbury,

drove one of the trolleybuses from the Market Place to the River Crossing. The vehicles were built by Brush of Loughborough, who were as pleased as the Derby folk that by 1934 the trams were on their way out and the Trolleys were in. In 1938 several of the new four-wheelers came into service. In 1947 the sliding skates which provided contact with the overhead cable were replaced with small track-wheels which reduced travel noise.

The last batch of trackless trolleys was built for Derby by Roe in 1960, featuring the advanced Sunbeam chassis, and two years later the Nottingham Road Depot closed and all trolleys then came from London Road. The winds of change were blowing through, and no-one was surprised when it was announced in the Evening Telegraph of August 2nd 1963 that the trolleys were to phased out, and diesel engine buses (the 'oilers' as their crews nicknamed them) would be used in their stead. There were emotional scenes when the last trolley was bid goodbye on its last journey by Mayor Coun Robert Francis Stott and his wife. When a diesel bus appeared it was booed by the crowd, in contrast to the cheers which followed the trolley.

There were a good many reasons why Derby abandoned its trolley policy, although the trolleybuses were not without their advantages.

This time we've turned from St Peter's Street to look down Babington Lane in the summer of 1964, with the van driver making a risky manoeuvre across the road. Looks as though he's gone off his trolley, although it does tell us 'Tern' on the frontage by Stevens, the men's outfitter.
The pedestrians in the middle of the road have some careful thinking to do, and the driver of the Ford Anglia, bottom left, is gunning his car out of the congestion.
You'll see we have caught St Peter's church on camera, behind and above the motorcyclist. The Wolsley vehicle on the right is of the model once used by the Derby police force, TRB meaning registered in Derbyshire. Excuse us now if we step back on the pavement.

Above: The Derby Electric Supply staff outing of 1956 was another very popular 'extended family' occasion for employees who worked together and because they were more or less of an age, socialised together. They are about to set off from the Full Street premises, which belonged to the power station, and all these seen here would enjoy a trip round the Derbyshire Peak District and remember the outing in fine detail - long afterwards... together with many others twixt Chesterfield and Buxton, Ashbourne and Glossop. At this southern end of the Pennine Range they would tell you that the highest point is Kinder Scout (2088ft). They will discuss the wonder of Chatsworth House and the Blue John mines (purple fluospar) at Castleton, all in their Derbyshire playground. Their work premises were demolished in the 1970s.

Some of it forms part of The Industrial Museum of Derby.

Right: Taken on The Cornmarket with St Peter's main thoroughfare on the left beyond the Wraith like Roller beneath the signpost. To the rear of the SOS 1939 bus there is Burtons the tailors in the background. In the days of the trolleybuses the taking of this tight corner would sometimes derail the trolley's sliders from the overhead power cables, so that the trolley arms would swing round violently and smash the large window, seen above the bus-driver's cab. The only answer was to hang something over the window to catch the arm ends and cushion them, so saving another expensive breakage.

Long before the days of the giant supermarkets, with their equally enormous car parks, proper shopping would take place in areas like this. For this was the Moreledge Open Market, seen here in the mid 1930s, just a couple of years after its May 1933 opening. At the time the market facility seemed very modern and well equipped. It compared well to similar market areas in neighbouring towns and cities, particularly in terms of its spaciousness and clean modern lines. A wealth of nostalgic information is contained within this delightful photograph; the fashions worn by the ladies in the picture were entirely typical of the time, with long skirts and coats complemented by stylish, closely fitting hats and the ubiquitous shopping basket. A motorbike and sidecar can be seen at the bottom right of the photograph, this was an affordable method of transport for mature motorcycle enthusiasts with growing families. The reign of the Moreledge Open Market lasted just over four decades and it was pulled down in August 1976. The new facility was located in the Eagle Centre. The old market site would later find a different use - as home to the local Magistrates Court.

WW Winter Limited

Above: *The Municipal aerodrome at Burnastone came into being as a response to enthusiasm in Derby for air status. As sometimes happens with matters of public transport, the market research was of the 'wing and a prayer' variety. On the airfield the propeller driven high wing Miles Marathon (left) and the low wing Dakotas make an impressive backdrop to line-up of pilots. aircrews and aerodrome officers who kept the whole enterprise looking good. If only the airfield had been longer, if only there had been room for regular runways long enough to take jumbo-jets. Lots of ambitious cities have believed that they could compete in the early scramble to become a national and then international airways enterprise only to find, like Derby, that there was a shortfall of resources, nearness to freight and volume of travellers to sustain non-stop flight schedules which alone makes such investment worthwhile.*

In the end Derby became part of the East Midland compendium and invested in the highly successful venture at Castle Donington, home of East Midlands Airways.

Right: *The first aeroplane to land at Derby was a Bleriot piloted by one B.C.Hucks who touched down on the Racecourse on July 11th 1912, and who gave a flying display that evening. From then an annual display took off. so to speak, organised by the Avro Aircraft Company, with pleasure flights at three guineas a time at the beginning, and taking off from the racecourse. It became so popular that the event was extended on to two weeks and the Town Council quickly got the message.*

The Manor Estate was purchased at Burnaston and Derby's first Lady Mayor Ald Elizabeth Petty cut the first turf on October 29th 1937. It was completed not much before the war started and the first plane to land there was on April 26th 1939. The RAF Volunteer Reserve had been interested for a year by that time.

The official opening was by Air Minister Sir Kingsley Wood before a crowd of 5000 on Sat June 17th 1939 which watched the magnificent display by Spitfires, Lysanders and Gloucester Gauntlets, Fairy Battle-bombers, Blenheims and Hampdens, the giant attractions of the day, a Hercules aeroplane of Imperial Airways and sight seeing flight tours over Derby.

The airport became a training 'drome for the RAF during the war. When it was handed back after the war it soon became Derby's Civil Airport and in 1946 an international air taxi service started. In June 1947 large crowds came to the air display which featured a 'Sky Chieftain' air-liner, which was in fact a converted Lancaster bomber, impressive nevertheless.

Flights started to Jersey in the Channel Islands in May 1953 by Dragon Rapide aircraft routed via the Birmingham airport. Derby Aviation used converted Dakotas to run its flight schedules as the aerodrome only had grass runways. The picture shows the flying personnel at Burnaston in the 1950. In 1964 Derby Aviation became British Midland Airways and moved to Castle Donington.

DOVEDALE

WW Winter Limited

Above: The changing face of Derby, seen here down King Street, is an astonishing tribute to those planners who had the courage to decide and to act their single-mindedness, demolished St Alkmunds, which would have been to the left of the construction ongoing here, and replaced it by St Alkmund's Way as the King Street underpass.

Right: Stationed on the Kennings showrooms forecourt in Queen St stand ten immaculate Land Rovers waiting for customers in the 1960s, when roads were obviously a good deal quieter. The building end advertisement linking Kennings with Austin and Nuffield was surely sound strategy, for Kenning was also a self-made man. He emulated Lord Nuffield who started his working life as Bill Morris. a canny young man who learned about cars as a mechanic and who did much to fill the roads of Derby and most other roads in Britain with cut-price Morris cars after the First World War.

WW Winter Limited

Measham Car Auctions, a comfortable drive from the centre of Derby, was the setting for this photograph. A 'Washmobile' automatic car wash had been installed and a delightful young lady, complete with fashionable hairdo from the time, was recruited to add a sense of glamour to the scene. The picture dates from around 1960 and its centrepiece is the shiny, smooth Renault Dauphine motorcar. Few examples of this progressive saloon survive to modern times, most have succumbed to the effects corrosion. They really were ahead of their time, not just in terms of styling, which was extraordinary, and included features such as rear engine, air cooling and spacious, beautifully crafted interior.

In the early 1960s a 'taxi war' broke out in London and the black-cabs rival mini-cab operators chose the cheeky Dauphine as the main weapon in their armoury. The publicity derived from their choice generated tremendous interest in these little cars as they soon became one of the top selling foreign cars on Britain's roads. The Renault gained an ill-deserved reputation for poor handling with drivers not used to rear-engined cars 'losing' the back end of the vehicle when attempting over ambitious cornering speeds. Overall the cars were wonderfully quiet and comfortable to drive in, with four doors and soft suspension making them a hit with drivers and passengers alike.

WW Winter Limited

WW Winter Limited

Above: It is still quite straight-forward to find a skilled chimney sweep in *the good old Yellow Pages* but this picture depicts a time when the chimney sweeping business operated on a much higher plane. *The Wright Chimney Sweeping Service* offered to clean your chimney or flue with either brushes or the new electric vacuum technique. It is understood that this service existed alongside a substantial haulage and transportation business owned and managed by the Wright family. Regular attention from the chimney sweep would help avoid those unexpected falls of soot that were capable of spoiling the whole day when they occurred, though sometimes a careless sweep could make almost as much mess himself if not careful! Most modern houses exist without the need to burn solid fuel and so visits from the *lucky*

chimney sweep few and far between. It is difficult to recall these times without remembering the performance associated with actually *lighting* those coal fires. What a job it was, dirty, fiddly and long winded. This picture is thought to have been taken on a street adjacent to the railway station.

Top: This is the sort of car service bay that owners dreamed about and the mechanics of 1955 could work in at maximum efficiency with all the testing and repair facilities in easy reach. It was a superlative publicity shot showing a faultless bay in which the owner felt certain the service would be well worth the money.

Rolls Royce was the image of aspiration in Derby, and the work force, though making aero engines, were well drilled in the importance of appearance, more than any other town probably; cars were invariably well turned out, and the car services were well rewarded in keeping them that way. The two-tone Vauxhall Velox, Derby registered, as shown in the picture understood to be in Oscrofts in Derwent Street, had appeal limited by and large to the women drivers. The consensus on shiny patent leather and two-tone shoes was that they made men look Yankee or gangsterish; but our wives and sisters thought them fashionable. Some of our well heeled Derby families were setting off with the children at this time to Disney World, completed in 1955.

Looking at the picture, remind yourself that nothing stands still. Already Brookside, which was along Markeaton Brook, had been 'uplifted' to become at this stage Victoria Street and the brook was no longer visible. When the Derby Hotel & Improvement Co. built the complex on the right culverts were put in to safeguard against the possibility of underground flooding. The memory of the steam roller which tippled into one of the culverts created much interest in the problem of retrieving it. The Brookside Presbyterian church was the first of three to be built here in 1784 in the Palladian neo-classic style. In the 1860s you would have found a very different church of Gothic architectural persuasion which encouraged a hundred years of worship until 1961 when it was demolished in favour of Ranbys store.

The third church, the United Reformed, is built into the Debenham redevelopment opened by the Lady Mayor Coun, Mrs Elsie Jane Mack in a civic service on 8th December 1963. "I heard Sydney Wooderson has just done a four minute mile, dad." "Near enough son, probably caught the trolley in the picture alright." "Get the toasting fork, Albert, and poke the fire, we're having toast and jam for tea." That's mum from the kitchen. Those were the days. Or were they... Not long before this photograph was taken the Prince of Wales, Prince Edward, who could have become Edward the VIII but was never crowned, came back from a holiday cruise with the twice divorced Mrs Wallis Simpson and had to face the choice of leave her; leave with her.

The Duke and Duchess of York became King George VI and Queen Elizabeth on Wednesday May 12 1937 and the people seen here with 500,000,000 others listening to their wirelesses everywhere heard the new King give his first broadcast to his people. 'One Crown. One Nation. One Empire'.

Shopping spree

From the vantage of Cockpit Hill this photograph shows The Old Morledge Market covered stalls and the non stall-holders making hard going of selling on a hazy lazy day in the summer of 1932. The men are generally behind the market, having driven the horse and cart from outlying areas and set up their wares for sale. Though the area of view shows mostly men, the covered stalls would tell a different story, of women buying thriftily, making low wages stretch as far as they would go.

The picture shows the Guildhall and All Saints on the skyline and to its right St Alkmunds, St Mary's, The Power Station. Beside the River Derwent is the old silk mill. The picture has an aura of anticipation, an opportunity to come into the modern world. The opportunity was seized and the new planners conjured The Council House The Court Houses and in the foreground possibly the best bus terminus in the kingdom.

WW Winter Limited

Above: It was true, and still is, that Currys had branches everywhere. This photograph was taken in Derby when the Company was a family business, with a powerful reputation for customer care. Set up in 1927, the firm sold bicycles in a big way. As a form of cheap transport they were popular and relatively safe. Everyone knew that if you said 'Sit up and Beg' you were answering the question, 'What kind of handlebars do you prefer', as against straight or drop-head.

The Company diversified, especially in towns and cities with many cobbled roads, and sold the wireless and gramophones to broaden their horizons.

'If you can find a better home, go to it,' seemed to be highly applicable to Currys, who were ever mindful of the shifting patterns of customers' retail shopping routes, which is how they came to open in Traffic Street but to outflank competition they have had to move again, both product and position, moving forward into promoting TV's, video cameras, video recorders, washing machines and almost any popular electrical household appliance. The two branches in present-day Derby are on the Kingsway Industrial Estate and at the Wyvern Retail Park, down the road from Derby County AFC's new football ground at Pride Park.

Curry's head office used to be in Ealing, London, but these days it's in Hemel Hempstead, and the Company is a part of the Dixon Stores Group. One thing hasn't changed, Curry's tradition of always believing that the customer's interests come first.

Below: Are you one of thousands of children who flattened their noses to Ratcliffes' toy shop window on a cold winter's night at the end of the 1930s ? This was just the place to drag your folks on a pre-Christmas practice run to get them in the right spirit, although times were hard for some. The toys seemed to be much more gender centred in those days with dolls, dolls' prams, dolls' clothes, dolls' houses and furniture, plus teddy bears for the girls and soldiers, cap guns, clockwork trains, toy cars and bows and arrows for the boys.

The emphasis of the sales drive was that British toys were best and that they should be rewards for good girls and boys.

So if your presents were made in Britain you'd been good and if you received anything else you weren't so good, according to Ratcliffes' advertising. Did it work?

It wasn't true, you were the one who wanted that special something, did you mind if it came from Huddersfield or Hong Kong? Did you even care if it came from Ratcliffes?

Below: St Peter's Street looking towards The Spot. Taken in 1948, this shows why the dramatic changes which have taken place were necessary, for here is a town of narrow street by today's requirements, crowded to distraction within the confines of its road frame.

The Wolsley is still with us at this time, an elegant car and one that felt rather like a bus to drive, easier when they had power steering. The trolley, which is serving a community out at Allestree, has suburbanised the village to Derby and changed their pattern of shopping. The post-war baby boom (over 20% higher than needed to maintain the status quo), the National Health Service that looks after you from cradle to grave, the comprehensive school based on ensuring equal opportunity for all; all this added up to this scenario and the need for action.

'The wind of change,' as someone said,'is blowing and it is easier to go with it than not.' Appropriately enough someone else said, 'If you don't want to come, get off the bus.' Very few ever do.

Right: St Peter's Street in 1959, looking towards the Spot from Babington Lane.

Just behind the Spot was Eastern's Art Deco establishment which specialised in the decorative art style of the period 1910 to 1930. This featured strong geometric motifs and patterns, powerfully bold, with primary or contrasting colour schemes.

To the rear of Eastern's is the vast Gaumont 'Palace' cinema where its theatre-goers were watching 'Ben Hur', starring Charlton Heston, and the Gaumont British News would be covering the worst fog for seven years, railway station closures and the arrival of the *Mini* car. Also Dior's 'Red Cabbage' dress. The Palace became the Odeon in 1961, just in time to report Soviet cosmonaut Yuri Gagarin's venture into space travel.

On the left-hand side of St Peter's Street is Halfords, the famous cycle shop, and if you come forward and cross the road to the right hand corner, there is The Benefit shop at the junction of Babington Lane with St Peter's Street, which offered the additional entertainment of the 'poles coming off the trolley buses' which is bit of shorthand that we think locals will understand.

WW Winter Limited

Left: Taking another walk along St Peter Street, the eroded pavements tell their own story of an affluent society with every kind of road transport from bus to Rolls Royce, from van to wagon, sports car to saloon, motor-bike to pedal bike, to foot power. On the right, one of Derby's most famous stores up to July 1970, a store which was the equal of any London department store in range and quality of products. It was the enterprise of two men, Harry Thurman and William Malin, who were both employed at George and George, the woollen and silk specialists.

When G and G closed in mid 1870s Thurman and Malin crossed St Peter's Street and set up their business in the imposing four storey premises which featured a frontage decorated with bronze which was always highly polished.

Business was rewarding at numbers 8 and 9 and their frontage grew into St Peter's church yard. The electric lift installed to all sales floors was an innovation which provided the right image of superior customer service, and in 1929 Thurman and Malins' store was celebrating with a grand golden jubilee sale which generated enormous sales.

Above: Although microchips had not been discovered in 1945, this is not to say that their possibility had not been thought of. Before the days of this picture in the Hazelhurst Ironmonger wireless service repairs room at 127 London Road taken during wartime, there were Crystal-sets, a type of broadcasting receiver which instead of valves uses a crystal or small piece of mineral ore which, by allowing current to pass through it in one direction only, changes the high frequency currents received on the aerial into low frequency capable of operating headphones. Some readers will recall the thin wire called the 'Cat's Whisker' used to make contact with the crystal. So the valve sets serviced at the Hazelhurst facility were, after all, only a passing phase between Crystal sets and the modern radio-receiver.

The repairmen have Edison to thank discovering the 'Edison Effect in 1884. which was the first step on the way to the invention of the two electrode wireless valve by Dr Fleuming and the triple electrode valve by Dr Lee de Forest. They are employed largely because of 'interference' which causes crackling. Their job was to find if this was coming from outside the set or inside. They would check to see if the set worked OK in the room they are in, in which case just the handling charge we hope. If it didn't they would routinely check the connections, valves, coils, pins and sockets. springs and switches, HT batteries, verdigris, dust, aerial wire, coil winding and if necessary, continuity throughout the set. They were wireless detectives so to speak.

Left: The photograph shows the trade counter in a Derby garage. In those days you could still go into one of these service stores and get almost any part for your car by just describing it (and you didn't have to buy the entire headlight housing to get the bulb). Times were changing fast, however, and it wasn't long before the independent car parts store was having to compete with the recycling of serviceable parts of crashed cars. Meanwhile the specialist parts suppliers for individual makes of cars continued to prosper.

Below: They were stirring times in 1945: whilst Prime Minister, Winston Churchill, declaring 'The War in Europe is at an end' on Sunday May 13, the East Midlands Gas Board was proclaiming 'All Gas Washing Machines Boil'.

This was an excellent strategy for after seven years of war, during which the nation had been directing its efforts to the war effort, it told the public that materials and manufacture for peace were now back.

Taking such a picture marked a new era of opportunity for the youthful Hubert King who later became an executive photographer at the Winters studio in Midland Rd.

The war had restricted the availability of photographic materials except for essential war work. The EMGB knew that war is a dirty business; that clean clothes make people feel good; that after VJ (Victory Over Japan) on August 14th, a million men would be demobbed within six months; and that once the celebrations and thanksgiving were over, there was going to be a lot more home washing done.

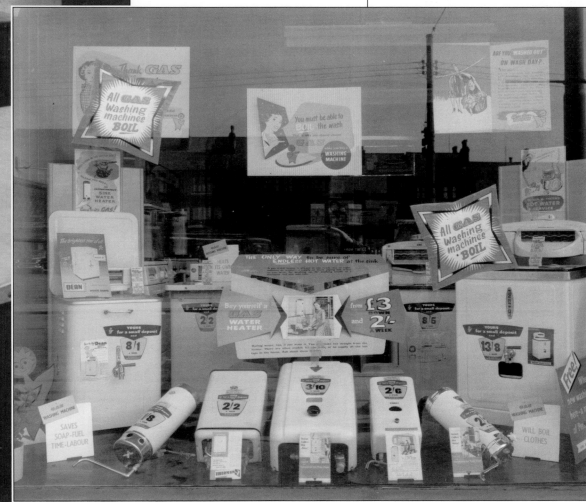

Above: Some remember him as the 'Take Your Pick' TV gameshow presenter Michael Miles, others as the man who said 'Right then. Open the Box,' as he put the key on top of the box chosen.

This keys us into the late 1950s and we are looking at a slice of Derby enterprise through the window of newsagent H Statham's at 39 Water Road, dressed to associate the show with Mars Bars. Something to eat whilst you're watching?

Mars goes on regardless of those who promoted it in the past, as have most of the other confections in this window display stacked with the 'spice' that makes viewing sweeter; Bounty, Maltesers, Opal Fruits and Spangles to name a few old friends - you can treat yourself today just as you did then. In 1959 two out three households owned the one eyed 'goggle box', as TV was sometimes called. On the larger world screen this was the time when the hovercraft moved into the news as a probability for conveying passengers on short inter-island and cross channel routes.

'Teenagers' were reckoned as a force by the marketing moguls in the year '59 after statistics published estimated they had a total of £800 million a year to spend and adverts began seriously 'putting on the Style' to win their custom.

Below: The Kingston Shop front window dressed for the 'Daily Express National Shop Window Display' competition is a mouth watering puzzle.

From the posters displayed it reasonable to suppose that from the unlikely message they carry, not only do you have NZ shepherds and sheep farmers for neighbours but the builders of refrigeration ships and road transporters and shop-store refrigeration plants, butchery department staff, newspaper proprietors and newsagents might also be smiling thanks to you at the end of the bus-stop queue or food chain. 'Helping your Neighbour' is a commendable sentiment but how about him dropping the price a bit and helping you. Charity is charity and business is business and competition is what measures staple product market-prices. The bottom line is 'There's no sentiment in business'.

Bottom: 'Position is everything' is a phrase remembered from the mists of time. Whoever first said it, it must have been remembered by shop owners thousands of times when they were going into new retail premises.

A few yards one way or the other and the customers can't get in through the door fast enough. The new Marks and Spencer opened on this site in October 1998 so it can't be such a bad situation on St Peter's Street. H Samuels the Jewellers moved to the corner of the Corn Market and Albert Street though. The clock which was is dedicated to Samuels looks like the one which used to tell the time above Jacksons, the 'all one price' shop.

If you were married about this time and are wearing one of H Samuels' wedding rings you'll know they were advertised as being lucky. We hope they were. Cox and Malin the wine importers have disappeared. We recall being told one of the owners died prematurely. The sign above on the Elizabethan style facade was splendid at night and gave the Irish stout drink prominence with the name Guinness flashing on and off arrestingly.

WW Winter Limited

Above: This is Green's Shoe Repair Shop in the London Road of Derby in the 1960s. Well known personalities hitting the headlines at the time included Marilyn Monroe, Sophia Loren and Christine Keeler. The famous and newsworthy, and all of them sharing the same foot-fashion as the model in this picture - stiletto high heeled shoes. Seeing there is no foot rest for trying on shoes at Greens we guess this is a mocked up publicity - picture to show where you could get a broken heel repaired, without hobbling home. What strengthens the contention is the seating, cigarette ashtray and 'Today' magazine which all suggest a short stop. The sales girl with her dance dress on is a novelty. Note that the seated lady is putting on her right shoe first, which is good, as our ancestors deemed it bad luck to put on the left shoe first.

Right: This is the lower part of St Peter's Street with the Midland Drapery on the right, a Company founded by Edwin Thomas Ann. A Welshman by birth in 1852 he came to open his store in Derby in 1882 in St Peter's Street. His business prospered and he expanded it into what was Bag Lane which was renamed East Street in the time of Queen Victoria. He was liked by those who knew him and respected by all. In due course he became an Alderman, and a Justice of the Peace. He was the Mayor of Derby in 1898-1899. and again in 1905-1906, and was knighted by King Edward VII in 1906. His ways were always courtly, and he greeted those who worked for him each day with a smile and a friendly word.

When he died in 1913 the street through which his funeral cortege travelled were lined with Derbeians, paying their respects as to a real friend and benefactor, for he gave many gifts to the town, not least of which was an ambulance. His emporium grew in four stages and was identified instantly by the image of a very large magnet, which did succeed in drawing the customers. When all the building was finished it had a frontage of 115 yards along St Peters and East Streets. For the ladies who worked at the store who lived out of town there was in store accommodation, and the men stayed at a London Road hostel. The store closed in the 1970s.

WW Winter Limited

In 1960 the East Midlands Gas Board decided to take the product it was retailing to the customer, and so had a showbus fitted out with the latest kitchen and bathroom gas appliances.
To admire the excellence of this presentation you will have to wait until it comes your way and step inside. It was a good idea as you will gather because it showed initiative by an up-to-date Company eager to serve you. On the down side it cost a lot to run including tying up stock of appliances, a driver and sales staff.
It made some sales yet perhaps because of the novelty of the vehicle. It served more as an invitation to see the full range in the proper showrooms and so never had full credit for the sales it generated.

WW Winter Limited

WW Winter Limited

believe it must be peace in our time," he said, waving the paper he had of his agreement with the German Nazi leader, Adolf Hitler.

'You mean we've just bought a new Murphy wireless with the unique alphabetical tuning system and you've ordered a new magazine, Mavis... what's it called... Picture Post.. .and it costs 3d a week ! Do you think we're made of money ?'
'Calm down Peter, for heavens' sake, that will only be half a new penny in 1971,' (when decimal coinage replaced the traditional 240 pence to the £).

Top: Campbells store at 31 London Road was the place to buy all furniture on the 'never-never,' starting with a deposit of twelve and a half per cent of the total and so much a week until the cash value plus the loan interest was paid off.

The great advantage to you was that you could enjoy the benefits of their excellent products before you had paid more than 2/6d in the £ of the total.

In those days, trades were not obliged to tell you what the on-cost was, but since money is the dearest thing you can buy, it's reasonable to imagine it would be fairly hefty.

The plus side for Campbell was that once you were making payments every week, the wise salesmen knew you would be a potential customer when the payments were coming to an end. Establishing buying by installments enabled everyone who was credit worthy to 'Buy now - pay later.' Campbells was flanked by Ronnie's antique shop whose goods for sale should therefore have been a hundred years old to be entitled to be called 'antique' in those days, on the other side Wilcox was a wholesale tobacconists.

Above: You have to believe that the Dalton's Wireless Store Manager was very pleased to have the new Murphy mains and battery sets for sale in 1938 as the war clouds gathered over Europe. This window is advertising the new style range, in which the sets look more like room heaters than the old Gothic- window design of wireless receiver. The advertising promised that you could find any station with the simplified method of ABC tuning, another small advance in the appliance of lateral thinking, and illuminated station search facility, from £7.00 to £13.50.

Did you stop up to hear the Joe Louis V Max Schmelling fight from the New York stadium on June 22nd 1938, when Louis floored Schmelling three times in the first round and then demolished him, revenge on the only man ever to beat JL up to then. Maybe you heard the news on September 3rd when Prime Minister Neville Chamberlain came back from crisis talks in Munich... "I

WW Winter Limited

MORLEDGE MARKET CELEBRATED THE 800TH YEAR OF ITS CHARTER IN 1954

And when they were weary of shopping customers could relax across the way in the Derwent Riverside Gardens, for if there is one thing Derby has always been good at, it's 'saying it with flowers'.

It had an underground store room too, used extensively during wartime: not many people knew that. It was also a good place for storing fruit to ripen for sale in the market. 'Pity it's all gone,' did you say? Well, it was a bit of a scrum when it rained or snowed so maybe the move to the Eagle Centre is a good thing. The market has been replaced by the new Derby Law Courts.

Above: The generous walk-way space around the perimeter of the old Open Market in the Morledge - a name which may be older than Derby itself - could be guaranteed to tempt shoppers to open their purses once they were in the complex of narrower inter-stall aisles. The fish market which was added was an immediate success.

Left: Now we're in the Morledge Market of 1954 watching the Mayor and Mayoress 'Beating the Bounds' in ceremonial celebration of the market in the 800 hundredth year of its charter.

Below: This crowded Derby shopping scene is capable of rekindling memories among those with a love of the city. The picture is dominated by the tangle of electricity cables positioned to carry the power for the trolley bus network. Beneath them the sign indicating the routes to Uttoxeter, Ashbourne and Manchester can be seen, fixed to one of the tall poles attached to the trolley cables. It is difficult to appreciate that the congestion caused to the centre of towns and cities like Derby before the 1960s occurred as a result of 'through' traffic destined for far flung destinations having to squeeze through the centre of most of the towns along the way. The age of motorways and inner relief roads would change all that from the 1960s onwards, making our town and city centres cleaner, healthier and safer. This view of St. Peter's Street shows *Maypole Dairies* and *H. Samuel's* businesses across the street from the camera.

Right: No one seems to be sure why the place where the subterranean conveniences were was called The Spot in the first place. The best explanation so far is that of the maltster who was showing a customer on his map where the Derby Malthouse was. 'There it is,' said he, pointing to where Osmaston and London Roads flow in and out of St Peter's Street, 'That's the very Spot!'

If you imagine a cross from corner to corner of the picture and look directly above its centre, you are looking at The Church of St Peter itself. X marks the spot in a manner of speaking.

You are about half a mile from the Royal Crown Derby Porcelain Company, which is near the Derby Royal Infirmary along Osmaston Road.

William Bemrose of Derby family printing fame is the one to thank for the great good which Edward Phillips and William Litherland brought to Derby, for it was he who refuted the rumours that the town would be covered by the ash from manufacturing salt-glazed earthenware, a very different process to that using the finest bone china as proposed by the two entrepreneurs. Together with chemist John McKinnes, Phillips and Litherland assured the populace that there would be no ash to smother Derby, and so were at last encouraged to set up their works. They received the Royal Warrant in 1890 and the Company has been proud to add the word 'Royal' to the famous 'Crown' granted as a marque earlier, which together make Royal Crown Derby Porcelain very special.

WW Winter Limited

Above: Believed to be the Qualcast Company's die-casting stores and warehousing of the 1940s, you're looking at another creditable example of the start-to-finish skill of Derby's heavy industries.

Since they were suppliers to nearby Rolls Royce they might have taken advice by the time this was taken, to take some of the back-ache out of the internal product, perhaps they moved straight on to fork-lift truck.

Certainly they moved into modern engineering design and marketing with their successful retail targeting for the 'Qualcast' lawnmowing units, by which time they had taken the back-breaking element out of the job.

Right: Thousands of Rolls Royce employees from the 1930s will recognise this view taken from Nightingale Road about six years before the outbreak of the 1939-45 war. The three well dressed drivers are evidently showing new trucks for moving products about the works. The public image of Rolls Royce is of perfect hand-built limousines. Phantom, Wraith and Ghost are examples of front-runners worldwide then as now, promoted by the sales drive of The Hon Charles S Rolls.

The automobile magic became reality when he teamed up with the all-time master of automotive design and engineering, Frederick Henry Royce. They set up in business in 1904 and moved to Derby together in 1908.

Sadly, Rolls died at 33 in an aeroplane crash, but his partner Royce went on to design and perfect the Rolls Royce 'Merlin' aircraft engines, powering the Hurricanes and Spitfires which outfought the enemy planes throughout the second world war. Imagine the proud drivers above responding a few years later, with the rest of a determined war-time work force, to Prime Minister Winston Churchill's moving appeal to 'Give us the tools, and we will finish the job'. During the war only one enemy bomber ever found the well camou-flaged Rolls Royce works. The German Dornier bomber came in broad daylight and as it passed over the works its open bomb doors were snared by a barrage balloon curtain. One bomb hit the Hawthorne Street entrance and one hit the stores. Finally other bombs hit houses near the factory before the bomber struggled free and fled.

From war-time invention came the founda-tions of our great Rolls Royce civil aero-engine industry which goes from strength to strength in Derby with the inflow of multi-million pound orders.

Looking again at the picture, some of you may also remember going to the Nightingale Junior School close by which was built to ensure a quality start for the children of the growing Rolls Royce workforce. It honours the name of 'The Lady of The Lamp,' as Florence is known for her habit of making night rounds to comfort the wounded soldiers in her hospital in the Crimea. This daughter of the Derby county family was responsible for the founding of schools of nursing in our

At work

Left: Foundry work was done by men as a rule, but some of the lighter operations could be handled better by women in the 1940s, if only because the tea had to be emptied from the packing cases before they could be used for product component part storage. The ladies all had their cups handy for the next mash when it was their turn to sit down.

Shoe boxes too had their part to play in the process, often used for temporary work-dockets, after the they were no longer required for shoes. When you bought new shoes you were always offered the box that went with them, which came in handy for keeping things together at home. Sewing materials come to mind, as well as cigarette cards, picnic sandwiches and love letters.

Below: Calendar printing at Bemrose and Son, who had works on Midland Road and off Nottingham Road. Here employees in 1959 are shown scrutinising calendars for the year 1960 to complete all the production stages for distribution and sales in good time, for there's nothing so dead as last year's calendar. Many people in Derby and its satellite villages have worked at Bemrose and Sons, whose investments in precision printing machinery paid off, for accuracy. honesty and quality product was guarantee of their integrity and value to the Company and to the Community. Security was tight, deadlines for print achievable within this serious business owned by a committed entrepreneur backed by a gifted family, and a dedicated workforce.

WW Winter Limited

'Loveliness is Yours if You use Snowfire Cream,' the makers of the famous skin treatment assured us, just the other day, or so seems. Here it is seen in the familiar aluminium containers on the conveyor system of F.W. Hampshire, a firm we are told began in the old Derby silk mill before it was established here in Sinfin Lane. The tins were packed in counter dispensers, which meant they were put under your hand on the chemists' counters for impulse purchasing, which was why they vanished so quickly perhaps; but more likely they called the product a 'Vanishing Cream' to sophisticate it as a cosmetic, rather than a treatment for dry hands.

The aluminium containers were only threepence, the opal jars (under the non-sticky, non-greasy label) were 1/6d in the shops. That's one new penny and six new pence respectively as from February 15th 1971. The Company, which serves the pharmaceutical industry mainly, has become Reckitt Toiletry Products Ltd. It is a manufacturing firm with an impressive record.

WW Winter Limited

Above: It's said that every picture tells a story and this one, which we believe to be in the accounts department of Power Samas in 1951, tells us that we had nothing to learn about the trend for open office planning.

The noise from the machines as well as the snap-cracking of the steam piped central heating would preclude conversation and once the operator was acclimatised, they would get on with the work because there was no alternative. Taken 48 years ago, this layout was the discipline of new technology about the start of the 1950, when it was usually the women who were the living 'computers' - Here they are

WW Winter Limited

programming cards with hole patterns which would tell the machines what to print as the old piano scroll told the pianola what keys to play, and as the Jacquard cards programmed the carpet looms to weave figured patterns over a hundred and fifty years ago.

Above right: Really moving with the times, the Derby Co-operative Society's new Model Dairy, photographed shortly after its opening on 14 September 1935, shows another big advance in specialised purpose-designed building, with a time and motion studied layout saving time, energy and labour. It was opened by Alderman W.R. Raynes.

The key elements in this picture show dependability, efficiency and cleanliness, plus the sky high emphasis on pasteurisation.

Most of us will rightly read into the 'Clean Milk' message the subliminal additional message 'in clean glass bottles', taken for granted.

Historically, the Derby Co-operative Society built its first dairy on Nottingham Road, Spondon in 1894 from which sales grew apace, so much so that after the end of the first World War the Society decided to build another, for which plans were submitted in 1921. These were turned down by the Council, amended and resubmitted in March 1922, completed and opened in 1923.

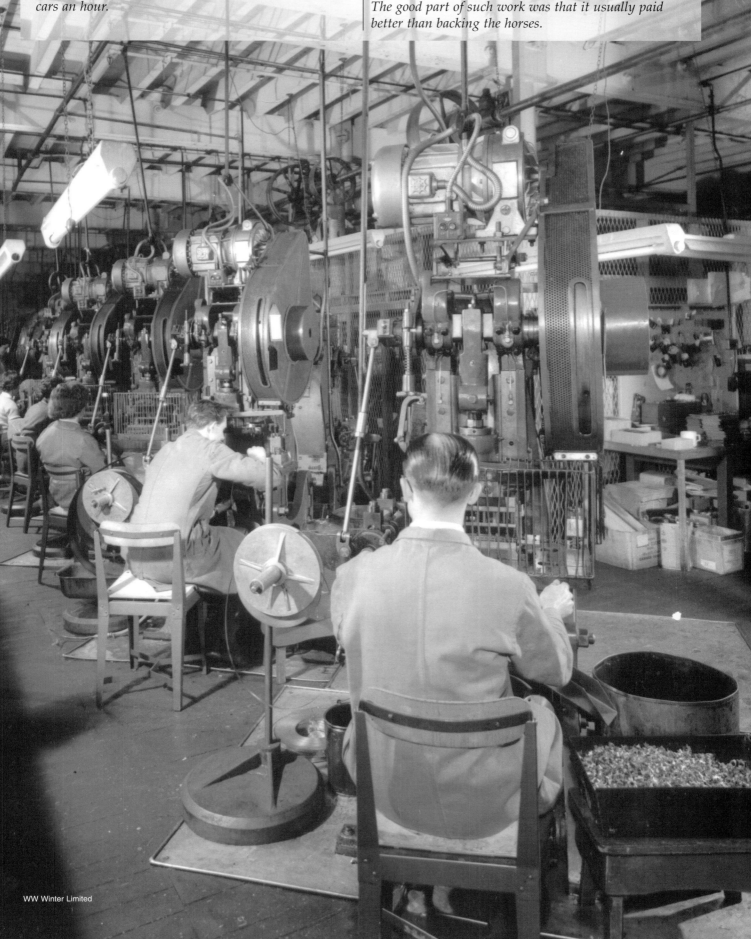

The psychologists amongst our readers will appreciate this shot of men hand finishing Pressac component parts at Long Eaton for the motor industry. One of the penalties of the car assembly line system was the need for remarkable efficiency of the suppliers, for to stop an assembly line could mean the loss of maybe a dozen cars an hour.

Given a concentrated attention span averaging 2.5 minutes before the mind needs change, even if for only for a moment, this kind of work suited people of placid temperament capable of self-programming to recognise any deviation from shape accuracy whilst they were weighing up which horse was going to win the Derby. The good part of such work was that it usually paid better than backing the horses.

Left: The Company which made the famous 'Pressure Cookers' in Derby was on City Road and also made saucepans and frying pans. All the manufacturing, assembling and despatch was carried out with a very strict quality control all the way through to labelling and packaging. We understand that the Company closed down, at least in Derby, but there was a Customer Care unit listed at lA Farrinton Close, Burnley, Lancashire in 1998.

Above: "Some talk of Alexander, and some of Hercules, of Hector and Lysander and such great names as these; But of all the world's great heroes there's none that can compare." A form of grenade was first used by Grenadiers attached to the Royal regiment in 1667 and the British army followed their lead in 1678. It wasn't only those who threw them who had to be accurate and well disciplined, but those who made them too. At this Derby munitions factory they had a production assembly line for making hand grenades during the war. There were different kinds and the type shown in the picture were Mills bombs which called for great care and precision in manufacture.

The grenades were used for clearing out enemy trenches and dug-outs or cellars where enemy soldiers might be hiding, or taking the tracks off tanks or damaging their vulnerable reachable parts.

The last line of the song where you began reading this relates to a famous British regiment, 'With a tow and a row and a towrowrow, of the British Grenadiers.'

Above: Here is a jolly picture of the women of Darley Abbey Cotton Mills; enjoying a compulsory photo session in the canteen are about 70 happy employees, all probably wondering why their break-time was being invaded and wishing they were out in the sunshine.

The mill was first built by Thomas Evans in 1782, on the River Derwent just North of the City Centre, and Evans was in partnership with Richard Arkwright, the famous Lancashire inventor, for a short time. In the winter of 1788 the entire mill was gutted by fire, and rebuilt the following year. Evans built a village around the mill which supplied a dedicated workforce until the 1960s. The Abbey house of refreshment was opened about 18 years later. The buildings were later re-ordered and utilised to established new Companies outreaching towards the next millennium.

Right: During the 1939-45 war period there were warnings on every hand that 'Careless Talk Costs Lives', according to the well remembered posters by Fougasse, and no one was more conscious of the message than the women of Derby who were on war work. (Pity the women in religious orders, though, after the rumour swept the country that German spies were masquerading as nuns, on the theory that no one looked at them on the streets.) So the girl friends and mothers who made these parachutes didn't talk about what they were doing until after the war and even then the habit of discretion gave little or no feedback for the record.

Derby was famous for its silk fabric manufacture, and maybe the oddest twist of all was that the method perfected in Derby is reported as coming from the observations of one John Lombe, an Englishman in Italy in the early 1700s. The upshot of this was The Silk Mill, purpose built by George Sorocold beside the Derwent, first of its kind in the country.

We are reliably told that the parachutes seen at the final inspection section of the factory were made from Fortison and were for dropping supplies from aeroplanes, but not people. It's possible that they were being made in Erasmus Street... if only the woman in white could speak.

Left: If this was your car in the Oscrofts repair section of 1955, we're sure you were highly satisfied with the service. Doesn't the sheer cleanliness and order convince you that this is a company to be trusted? It was part of the Kennings set-up of course, so would be subject to the same hands-on disciplines and workforce smartness.

It's said there is no gain without pain, and this picture is mindful in a way of going to the dentist. 'Open wide,' says the mechanic who looks sharp enough to be the manager, and runs a bead of weld along the chassis, whilst the car clenches its windscreen wipers together in pain. 'All finished' you can hear the MIG operator saying as he reholsters the gun and parks the face shield; 'Didn't hurt a bit, did it!'

Below: Here is another part of the Kenning success story in Derby, when this delivery man was walking up the drive with a tank full of paraffin on the end of his pipe. Well, if you remember, Kenning did promise a home delivery service years before when he himself worked in the market. The picture would be taken at about the time the Clean Air Act was coming into force - not very popular in the coal mining areas, but a sign of the times. If you remember the poisonous fume-laden smog caused by mill chimney emissions and open fire days in the days of solid fuel, then you'll be glad of Kenning's enterprise as an important advance towards central-heating options.

WW Winter Limited

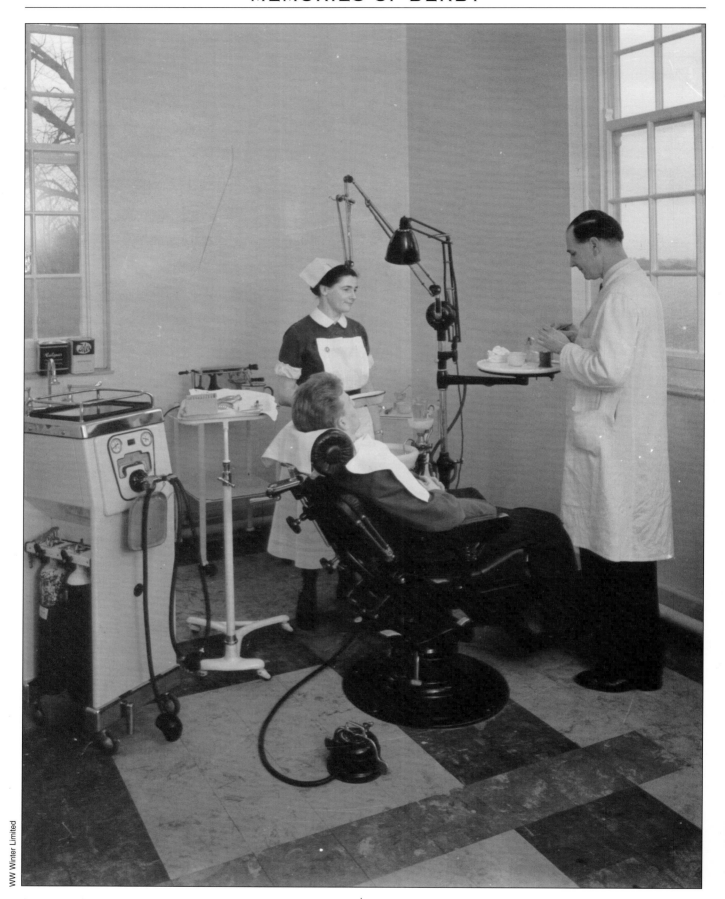

WW Winter Limited

Above: There is no other clue to this photograph. other than it was taken in the dental department of the Pastures Hospital at Mickleover. So we can only presume it was taken to indicate the high standard of medical care enjoyed by the patients in 1958. The Pastures was once the name of a mansion which belonged to the Heathcotes who lived in this area before they went South to live.

Then the Blanes lived there, and after that it was bought by Sir Abraham Woodiwiss who was twice Mayor, first in 1888, and then at the time of Queen Victoria's state visit in 1901.

Tatlers the printers

In 1926, the year of the General Strike, Mr. William Tatler and his son Jack set up in business together. Mr. Tatler senior had recently sold a pottery in Stoke-on-Trent and had planned to retire. Unfortunately he was defrauded of the proceeds of the sale and, when his son left school they decided to work together as jobbing printers. They already had connections with the printing trade through relatives at Cheadle in Staffordshire. Initially they worked from home: 234 Burton Road, Derby where, together with wife and mother Rose, they soon established a thriving business. Inspired by a small pocket diary that Rose bought in a corner shop they succeeded in selling their version to a high street chainstore - so starting a connection which still endures. Being letterpress printers they used handset type and treadle presses, a very labour intensive method with most operations performed by hand.

The business moved to its present premises, which had been built as a silk mill and previously used as a bottling factory by Burrows & Sturgess, in Abbey Street in the mid thirties. War time was difficult but conditions rapidly improved when the war ended and a Linotype (which did away with most hand setting of type) and powered platens were installed.

Trading at first as J. M. Tatler, the present company, J. M. Tatler & Son Ltd., was formed in

1963 shortly after Jack's son Robert entered the business. His son, another Will, has recently joined - the fourth generation of the family. Nowadays the great majority of work is printed offset litho, although the older letterpress machines still come in useful at times and other work is output digitally. In recent years the company has enlarged its premises and invested in the latest equipment in the belief that modern technology allied to a skilled, highly trained and flexible staff will enable it to survive and continue to prosper.

The first William Tatler would be amazed to see the computers that generate digital artwork for the work the company now produces but he would be delighted that there are still customers he dealt with on the books.

Today, as well as many personal customers the company produces high quality work for many local businesses, local organisations and design agencies but also has long standing customers in many other parts of the country.

Above left: Mr. Tatler senior, who together with his son, Jack, founded the business. *Above:* A Columbian press from 1849. *Left:* An early invoice which was used by the company in the 1920s.

234, Burton Road,
DERBY

Mr 192

DR **J. M. TATLER.**

PRINTER.
Letters and circulars a speciality
Orders executed at shortest notice.

=====================================

Date £ s. d.

The firm in focus for over 130 years

Well respected local photographers W W Winter Ltd were established when photography was in its infancy and the Company has become a unique mix of the old and the new. William Walter Winter, a Norfolk man, set up his business in 1864 in Midland Road, before relocating to its present day premises in 1867 on the opposite side of the road.

Henry Isaac Stevens, a renowned Derby church architect who was a friend of Winter, designed this purpose built studio. The importance of the building has just been recognised nationally by being declared a listed building of special architectural and historical interest.

It was built with a row of large church-like windows along its length. Because at this time there was no such thing as electronic flash, studio portraiture relied solely upon natural daylight. The studio was designed to face north to protect it from direct sunlight. Even then, so much depended on the weather. On very dull days, photography became very difficult.

Winter became a member of the Derby Photographic Society, which was founded in 1884.

In the mid 1880s disaster struck the premises when fire gutted the Midland Road Studios. After the fire, Winter took the opportunity to re-organise the building; a new studio and artist's room were added. The building then contained 30 rooms in all including some galleries where paintings and porcelain were exhibited.

William Henry King joined the company in November 1896 as a

Above: *William Walter Winter, founder of the company.* *Below:* *A rare picture of the studio taken in 1896.*

photographic assistant, operator and retoucher. With the help of Mr King, Winter became one of the pioneers of flash powder photography making photography of large building interiors possible. The portrait studio was revolutionised with the installation of carbon arc equipment made by Davis of Derby the Electrical and Mining Engineers. The electricity was produced by a small generator in the stables that were at the rear of the premises, making Winters one of the first company's to have electric lighting in Derby.

By now Winter's reputation had spread, becoming a photographer to the Royals and in particular King Edward VII.

In 1904, Mr King became the General Manager and in 1910 he formed a partnership with Mr H B Sheppard and, together, they bought out Mr Winter, who then emigrated to Canada where Winter was ordained as a Minister of his local church and died in 1925.

In 1930, Mr Sheppard sold his interest in the business to Mr King.

After World War II, in 1947, Mr King's son, Austin, became Managing Director before being succeeded by Mr W H King's grandson, Hubert King in 1975. Hubert, a member of the British Institute of Professional Photography for 40 years was given a Presidential Award by the Institute for Long and Distinguished Service in November 1986.

W W Winter's long history is a tribute to its continuing high standards. It has successfully managed to keep pace with the technical changes which have occurred in photography since the very early days. Led by Hubert King, the present employees respect the time honoured traditions of service and quality. Ever mindful of technical advances the Company has kept pace with technology through to present-day computers and digital imaging.

Above: The studio at the turn of the century.
Left: An interior of the studio, with a young Winter standing with the camera.

A household name in care and commitment

Walbrook Housing Association Ltd have a commitment to provide good quality housing that takes into account the emotional, physical and social needs of every individual.

It was an act of generosity coupled with the volunteer spirit of a keen group of Derby people that, back in 1966, set off the chain of events that was to link two homeless families with local people who were prepared to lend out two vacant houses.

The mid sixties was a time of growing need for housing in the Derby area. Concerned about the needs of the homeless and poorly housed, the ten local residents set up The Walbrook Housing Association in June, 1966. Deposits were made on a number of small terraced houses - a result of their fund raising activities - and mortgages were arranged with the Woolwich Building Society or with the City Council.

Things snowballed from there, and within two years Walbrook were able to extend their services and offer bedsits for young single mothers and their babies, and for a number of apprentices from the Rolls-Royce organisation.

Over the following years the number of properties Walbrook was able to offer for rent had grown to 20, and in 1970 their first group home was opened in response to a real need for a base where young single people could live together as a family unit.

It was time to set up a base for the Association to work from, and for one day a week potential tenants were interviewed in the front room of a house in Dairyhouse Road. Accountant and businessman John Blackton was appointed as Chairman, and a part time rent collector became the group's first employee.

Within three years Walbrook had doubled the number of rental properties. The group had a real breakthrough when the 1974 Housing Act was introduced, for the first time making available a Housing Association Grant (HAG) plus access to loan finance from the Housing corporation. Two more members of staff were appointed, a Development Director and a Secretarial Assistant. A few months later Walbrook Housing Association was registered as a charity, and more office space was found to deal with the extra responsibilities of administration and planning.

A new scheme got underway to provide housing for vulnerable mothers with babies. Each family in the house had their own bedroom and kitchen, but shared bathrooms and other facilities. The scheme gave the women and children the opportunity to make new friends who could support each other, while at the same time providing them with the privacy they needed. The scheme worked well.

With Janet Hammond appointed as the Association's Director and Secretary and Sandra Noon in the position of Housing Manager, homes were for the first time designed to suit the special needs of the wheelchair user. Janet's fundraising abilities became legendary, and the Association was able to furnish the nine flatlets for single mothers with babies from the proceeds of Walbrook's charity shop in Derby.

With the further expansion of the charity's operations, the need for more office space became pressing, and two houses in Curzon Street were converted to become the new headquarters. Janet was a woman with wide vision, and a number of new projects quickly followed: the Association opened a group of flats that would allow those with mental health problems to live in the community; in addition they began to look into the housing needs of the physically disabled, and they also took over the management of Ilkeston Elderly Persons Homes Association. The Disabled Persons Housing Service was set up in 1985 to help those who had a housing problem due to disability. A small team of dedicated workers pull together the skills of architects and occupational therapists, addressing a wide variety of the specialist needs of people with a disability. Training people towards independent living has formed a large part of the scheme. Many of those involved have in the past largely depended on the care of others, and a training flat has been furnished and equipped to enable them to try out new aids and equipment, some of which is designed and made to suit their own individual requirements. A person will often stay in the flat for a few days to become used to the practicalities of living alone, perhaps for the first time. Since it was first set up, DPHS has given independence to more than 2,000 disabled people.

*Facing page: Janet Hammond, Founder Member of WHA. **Facing page bottom:** Before Mr and Mrs Soloman Grant arrived in 1978 Walbrook had only been able to offer short-term lettings. **Above:** Owfields Almshouses in Ashbourne, built in 1640, and given a new lease of life for the 21st century by Walbrook Architects.*

It would have been easy during all the new developments and the forward planning to neglect the human touch, and Janet Hammond's policy was to make sure that each person housed by Walbrook can relate to at least one person within the organisation. She quickly realised that it is the small things that are appreciated, such as making sure that a person is actually taken to see a house rather than just being sent off with a key. Rent collectors were encouraged to chat and maybe find time to have a cup of tea with tenants they visited, as for many tenants the rent collector might have been the only other person they'd have spoken to that day.

The Association's growth and development over the last thirty years has meant that the services they offer today are wide and far-sighted. Today, properties in Derbyshire and Staffordshire are built or improved both for rent and for sale.

An appeal for the setting up of a Radio Warden Service was launched in 1983, with a view to linking older and more vulnerable people with a warden by way of a mobile radio alarm system. Incredibly, only a year later local residents and industries had raised the necessary £7,400 needed, and the scheme was set up.

Still with the elderly and the disadvantaged in mind, Walbrook's Care and Repair programme was set up to enable elderly owner-occupiers to remain in their own homes. The scheme owes much to the financial support of friends, and as usual within the Association, every penny has been made to work hard. Volunteers in their Handyperson Service provide home decorating, skilled joinery and other services. Repairs and renovations to older properties are looked at, costed, planned, and undertaken. When a major upheaval is necessary, temporary rehousing is provided for the occupants. This programme of ongoing improvement has meant that residents who prefer to remain where they are, have been able to stay within their own community among familiar faces and well-known streets. Acting as agents for Derby City Home Safety Campaign, Care and Repair also began to provide smoke alarms and security locks for elderly people, largely in response to referrals from the police, Social Services or Victim Support.

The phenomenal growth (now nearly 3,000 properties) and success of the Walbrook Association has been due to a combination of input from a caring and dedicated staff and a lot of generous support from their many friends. Walbrook has a well deserved pride in retaining its original inspiration and continuity of care and commitment, and not only looks back to a successful past but has a clear vision for the future. They look forward to the opportunity to continue to be a leading provider of high quality housing, care and support services in the East and West Midlands and Yorkshire.

Below: In 1985 John Blackman (Chairman), Richard Best (Director) of the National Federation of Housing Associations watch a tenant turn the key of Walbrooks 1000th home.

Old Ideals New Ideas

Jewellers W.E.Watts, founded in 1858, has been situated in St James Street Derby since 1939. Prior to this it was situated in the Market Place and before that St Peters Street. As can possibly be seen from the photograph of old pocket watch dials and boxes, W.E.Watts in the distant past has had branches in Nottingham, Chesterfield and Sheffield.

Today the business is owned by two families and is run by director Glyn Smoothy. His father, Frederick Smoothy, who ran the business before him, instilled the importance of traditional standards of Service

W.E. Watts are one of the few remaining jewellers to still have a resident watchmaker. The staff all undergo a two year National Association of Goldsmiths course to learn all aspects of the retail jewellery trade. Mr Smoothy himself is a qualified N.A.G registered valuer.

Certain aspects of the shop haven't changed and if you walk into W.E.Watts now you will still find old fashioned tills where the draw pulls through the hand written till rolls.

However other parts of the business are computerised and the management are constantly considering new concepts and ideas.

Although fashions in the jewellery trade are constantly undergoing subtle changes W.E.Watts attributes its long standing success to always having a broad base of both traditional and modern fine gold jewellery and diamond rings, Also a balance of both traditional Swiss watch brands such as Omega and Rotary combined with the new up and coming brands such as TAG Heuer and Maurice Lacroix.

Left: This envelope contains certification of an engagement or wedding ring made from newly mined virgin gold in the 1930's.

Below : W.E. Watts as it would have looked prior to modernisation in 1970.

Below Left: Old W.E.Watts pocket watch dials and boxes.

"Covenant" (Regd)

Engagement & Wedding Rings

Ordinary Rings contain gold obtained from second-hand articles of jewellery, dental plates, etc., with all its possibilities of an unhappy or sordid history.

"COVENANT" Engagement and Wedding Rings are the ONLY Rings guaranteed to be made from newly-mined gold never previously used.

"COVENANT" Rings can only be obtained from :

W. E. WATTS, Goldsmith, 9, MARKET PLACE, DERBY.

120 years of Standard Manufacturing

St Alkmund's Churchyard in Derby was the site of the first Standard Manufacturing Company, founded in 1877, but by 1906 the company were operating from the stately and rather elegant premises of Ye Old Moot Hall in Irongate.

It was at the Royal Agricultural Society's 1881 show that Standard Manufacturing first introduced the tree pruner that became famous all over the British Empire. Pruning was a dangerous occupation that had over the years produced its fair share of serious accidents, most of them being due to the fact that pruning trees had always depended on the use of long ladders. The 'Standard' pruner, which was operated from ground level, turned a dangerous job into what could be regarded as merely healthy exercise, and the tool took off in a big way. Inevitably, the enormous success of the pruner called forth a number of cheap imitations. But it was their competitors' use of the name 'Standard' that really made the company see red; after all, they had used the name for the last 25 years. Their catalogue issued a timely warning to the British public against buying the substandard articles. Interestingly, a similar situation exists today when cheap imports present a threat to the company's sales figures.

1906 saw the Royal Agricultural Society's third visit to Derby, and Standard Manufacturing took

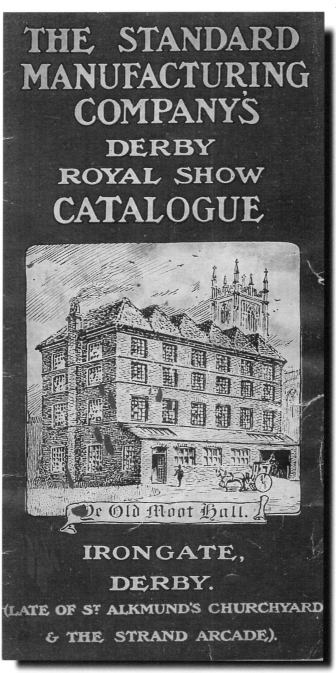

THE STANDARD MANUFACTURING COMPANY'S DERBY ROYAL SHOW CATALOGUE

Ye Old Moot Hall.

IRONGATE, DERBY.
(LATE OF St ALKMUND'S CHURCHYARD & THE STRAND ARCADE).

the opportunity to exhibit what was even at that time a large assortment of agricultural tools for use in gardens, orchards, farms, pleasure grounds, parks and woodland. As well as horticultural tools, their catalogue also included an extensive range of leisure items such as sunshade holders that could be screwed permanently to garden seats, fishing rod supports, ornamental tables, lawn games, fruit and flower gatherers and weed destroyers. An invention that would hold a large umbrella over an open carriage was, no doubt, a positive luxury to the occupants (and possibly the coachman?) in a shower of rain. The catalogue assures the customer that the device had been 'tested in the most stormy weather experienced in England.' A testimony indeed!

Things have moved on rather since 1881, and although pruners still feature largely in Standard Manufacturing's catalogues - in fact today they are the only company in the UK who manufacture pruners - today's designs and materials are vastly different from those employed 100 years ago. Specialist pruners are produced for a wide variety of different tasks. Lightweight tree pruners with a silver anodised alloy shaft and a rod and lever action have been designed to reach inaccessible places from ground level; easy-reach pruners are constructed in sections can be easily assembled into 6' or 9' lengths; telescopic pruners with a saw attachment can be adapted from light to heavy duty use. Added to the range the stylish

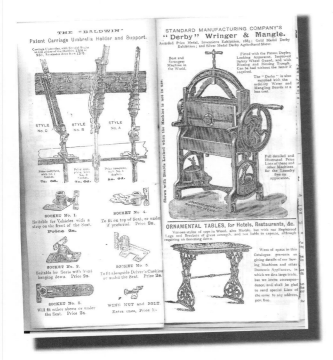

Things have not always run smoothly for Standard manufacturing, however, and over the years they have had their setbacks. The breakup of the British Empire, for example, has meant a loss to the company of their traditional markets.

New product development figures largely on the company's list of priorities. New innovations are an important part of their plans, particularly those that cater for the needs of the older generation, who often enjoy gardening yet have physical limitations that prevent them from pursuing their hobby.

It is natural for such a long established company to be optimistic for the future, and Standard Manufacturing intend to expand their operations, continuing to make quality British tools and to expand and enlarge the range of their products.

modern catalogue now offers a wide variety of fruit pickers, loppers and pruning saws.

Almost 120 years of engineering expertise is revealed in the products Standard Manufacturing have developed, and the company aim to give their customers quality and durability. This in itself, however, presents its own problems; the quality of the aluminium and steel used tends to be so good that the tools never wear out! The high standards the company has always held were reflected way back in 1895 when they were appointed as Makers and Purveyors of Horticultural Implements to Queen Victoria.

Top left: *Double page inside the Standard Manufacturing catalogue showing a Wringer and Mangle which was awarded a prize medal at the Inventions Exhibitions, 1885; a gold medal at Derby Exhibition; and a silver medal at Derby Agricultural Show.* *Below:* *Today, an exhibition for Standard Manufacturing Co showing various horticultural, agricultural and garden tools.* *Facing page:* *The Standard Manufacturing catalogue from 1906, printed for the third visit of the Royal Agricultural Society of England to Derby.*

The go-ahead company numbers among its customers garden centres, mail order outlets and catalogues such as Argos, and huge multiples like B & Q. They export to the USA, Europe and Hong Kong - in fact twelve and a half percent of their turnover is from overseas.

A family service of tradition and respect

Since cabinet maker George Wathall made the natural progression to undertaker, five generations of the Wathall family have been involved in the business.

The present firm was founded in 1858, and G Wathall & Son's offices were based at their first Green Street premises for around 70 years. Since then the firm has had a number of premises, with offices in London Road, Gerard Street and Normanton Road before they moved to Macklin Street at the turn of the century. The firm's Head Office is still sited there today.

The two world wars were not easy times for the funeral director. During World War I the best of the company's horses were commandeered to help the war effort, and their fleet of motor vehicles was badly hit by petrol shortages during the second world war. At that time the firm became part of a wide plan that involved Derby funeral directors in preparations for the possibility of large air raids on Derby. A temporary mortuary was prepared in premises in Abbey Street, and G Wathall & Son held extra coffins in stock for the duration of the war.

George Wathalls sons Will and Harry were left to take over the running of the business at a very young age, and continued to build up the name and reputation of the long-established family firm. Impressive and dignified, the funeral directors would walk respectfully ahead of the horse-drawn hearse or the shillibeer - a hearse and carriage combined. When motor vehicles came into vogue many people must have regretted the passing of the beautiful black Flemish horses that drew the hearse and the mourners' carriages.

Wathall & Son were a farsighted and progressive firm, however, and they were one of the first undertakers in the area to retire their horses and embrace the changes. This meant, of course, that the old stables at Macklin Street had to be converted to garages. The changes involved were vast, but the conversion was long-lasting, as the layout of the garaging remains exactly the same today. Wathall & Sons now have a fleet of discreet Daimler hearses and limousines as well as several other vehicles.

As would be expected from a company that was founded in the last century, the firm has seen many changes. In 1961, for example, the country saw a nationwide 'flu epidemic that had wide ranging and devastating effects. The company's work, of course, increased during the time of the outbreak, and Bill Wathall introduced innovations that changed their way of working, and the system used today is based on the changes he introduced at that time.

The company's practice was to make all coffins on the premises, and it was as recently as the 1980s that the machinery was taken out and coffins began to be bought in, though the lining is still done on the premises.

In the 1950s, Bill Wathall joined the business, enabling his father and uncle to relax a little over the years. Will and Harry retired in the 1970s. Bill became a qualified member of the British Institute of Embalmers and worked for the firm for over 40 years, eventually becoming Company Chairman. He was a well-known figure in the area, and would often give talks to local groups about his work. He was still working at the time of his death in 1995.

John Coulby, the present Managing Director, has been with the company since 1964, and worked alongside Bill until his death. Mrs Jean Wathall, Bill's wife, is now Company Chairman, and his daughter Helen Johnson, who joined the firm in 1985, is now the company secretary and works full time in the office. A total of 15 dedicated staff keep the company running in a smooth and dignified way.

George Wathall would be proud of the continued success of the company that he founded 140 years ago. Pre-paid funerals were unheard of back in those days, but the firm has now been offering the facility for a number of years and in 1995 Wathall & Son won the Golden Charter Funeral Planner of the Year Award for outstanding service, beating 1,900 other independent firms. A great honour for the company.

Wathall & Son's aim is to continue to offer the kind of traditional service it has always given to the people of Derby, while hopefully remaining a true family firm for many generations to come.

Facing page: William Henry stood by the door of the funeral warehouse on Gerard Street.
Below: Advertisement which dates back to 1912 at their branch on Green Street.
Right: Letterhead from 1936.
Below: Funeral procession 1940's passing through Derby market place.

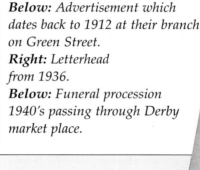

Switched on to success

WJ Parry & Company began its existence in 1942 as a partnership between Jack Parry and Henry Martin, both of them employed by Ericsson's Telephones Ltd. They set up their business on a part time basis in small, scattered buildings at Beeston, Nottingham, sub-contracting for coil windings used in telephone relays.

Progress up to 1945 enabled the two partners to concentrate full time on their new company and convert to a private limited company. From then onwards coils for customers in the telephone industries and football turnstile counting equipment predominated in company ledgers.

In 1948 the inconvenient Beeston Works were abandoned and the move made to Victoria Mills in Townend Road, Draycott. Only three out of 28 rooms there were available but as the rest were vacated Parry's took them over until they eventually bought the whole mill. This had been a difficult decision, but one necessary to the future of the company. Those were days of fierce competition in the lighting industry, and it was clear that the choice was to expand or be squeezed out of business by other companies. A little cost cutting was necessary, and Parry's began firstly by buying in the best coil

winding equipment possible, and then by looking closely at the assembly line and changing operations to fit flow-line methods.

The innovations paid off, and within the space of two years Parry's were the largest independent producer of discharge lamp control gear in the UK, employing 370 people at Draycott and 100 at Stapleford, where Parry's Mechanical Engineering Department were marketing a range of fancy goods

In the late 60s Parry's set up a new development section, and exciting new innovations in fluorescent lighting were made, which enabled fluorescent tubes up to a length of 4ft to be used in boats, caravans and public transport from 6, 12 or 24v accumulators.

Expansion and diversification was on the cards, and in the late 1960s the company took over a knitwear company in the mill and ventured into the production of knitwear for all the family. Success seemed assured for some time but unfortunately by January 1971 knitwear orders were thinning and the shortage of work led to redundancies. A month later the knitwear division closed down.

such as letter racks, nests of trays and fruit baskets under the 'Artstyles' name, as well as supplying parts for domestic equipment. It was not long before the company's output had increased 17 times - with a workforce that had merely doubled.

The appointment of a Sales Manager meant that a determined push to export was made. The company faced strong competition from Continental manufacturers who were already established. With the backing of the Board of Trade, Parry's began to exhibit at the Gothenburg Light Show and Hanover International Trade Fair. An integral unit for a mercury vapour lamp proved to be a particular success. The easily-fitted unit did away with the need for large numbers of conventional lighting in premises such as garages and workshops. The firm's hard work paid off, and substantial export orders began to come in from Portugal, Sweden, Southern Ireland, Singapore, Australia and Jamaica. Record sales both at home and abroad were reached and within a few years the company had doubled its export figure for the second year running, announcing export sales of £500,000.

Above: Victoria Mills seen from the air.
Facing page, top: Jack Parry, far left and Mr Henry Martin, second right, co-founders of the company.
Facing page, bottom: A 1940s view of the premises.
Below: A wintry photograph from the 1940s, the Directors car park is where the house stood.

equipment and selling through distributors to pubs, motorway service areas and thousands of small catering establishments nationwide. In spite of the climate of recession, sales continued to rise, and the equipment was exhibited at Hotelympia, a bi-annual event at Olympia, aimed at the Catering and Hotel industry.

In the mid 1970s W J Parry Domestic Products Ltd had set up a plant in Pinxton to produce energy-saving vacuum cleaners. These were light in weight, and were given the descriptive name of Light n' Easy.

The mechanical side of the business, however, was doing very well. The company's main works at Draycott had four floors totalling 100,000 sq ft of working area. The tool room and press shops were housed there, as was the lighting products assembly. 1970 saw the concentration of the business at the Draycott factory, and the electro plating plant at Nottingham Road Stapleford was sold off.

Business in Australia was growing, and exports to the country had totalled around £90,000 in 1972. Before long, plans were afoot to set up a new manufacturing subsidiary in Australia. The developments followed Parry's growth in South Africa, when Parry South Africa Pty Ltd was established to manufacture and assemble parts.

After a temporary lull in orders which meant that workers' hours had to be cut, the success of Parry's picked up, and through the 1980s it was a case of 'all systems go' as business boomed. The streamlined and fully automated Victoria Mills PARMAR plant at Draycott continued to develop its fluorescent units for homes and offices, and its sodium and mercury vapour control gear for works and street lighting. The new London Bridge, built around 1980, was lit using control gear from Parry's. More than a million complete units were produced every year, and it was Parry's aim that every single component of each individual unit had a proved performance. They were guaranteed in all conditions.

The continued success of the company meant that a good number of jobs were on offer in 1974, and Parry's found themselves advertising for press tool makers, labourers, draughtsmen, assembly workers to assemble control gear, and clerical workers. Buses carried workers from a number of outlying areas to and from the factory in Draycott.

In 1972 the company purchased (Ridgeway) Catering Equipment Division, making fryers, bain maries and servery

By the 1980s, electronic components were an important addition to the gear made by Parry's, and recognising the future potential in electronics, the firm expanded into premises on the other side of the road.

The modern single-storey 14,000 sq ft building was developed especially to manufacture electronic items. The final stage involved landscaping the development. Sixty trees and 150 shrubs were planted in an attractive layout which would screen the new works site.

The space vacated in the main works was put to good use, and the catering equipment division was expanded. Gas griddles and chargrills, food displays, heavy duty fryers, pizza showcases and coffee machines were just a few of their products, and an experienced sales team was there to provide advice on the planning of restaurants, pubs, cafes and clubs.

Parry's dedication to developing user-friendly designs, simple plug-in systems and their reputation for quality at competitive prices won them global recognition. The heavy duty design, the sleek, attractive looks and a design aimed towards the elimination of grease and dirt traps attracted attention, and in the mid 1990s Parry Catering Equipment Ltd was awarded the prestigious award BS5750, which was presented to the company by Kenneth Clarke who was then Home Secretary.

Room was left on the new site to more than double the works area and to erect an office block, and this work was completed in the 90s and continuing success of Parry of Draycott has virtually assured future expansion.

A new division, PARMAR Distribution supplying Lighting Control Gear to the wholesale trade, began trading in 1992 and subsequently a London Branch was opened in April 1996. At the present time, half a million items, from the smallest lamp clip to the most modern High Frequency Dimmable Ballast are in stock at any one time, and their glossy catalogue details hundreds of products.

In June 1997 the Lighting Control Division and the Mill were sold to an American Company, ADLT, and W.J. Parry relocated to the New Factory across the road and the Artstyles Division moved to Castle Donington.

Parry's have long had a determination to be the first in the field with production techniques, new developments and innovations, while at the same time maintaining quality and increasing capacity. The company look forward to the future and to further developments - and the opportunity to continue meeting their customers' expectations at fair prices.

Above: The new premises built in 1982 and extended in 1997. Facing page, top: Salvage operation in the Mill following a fire in the mid 50s. Facing page, bottom: A late 1950s staff photograph.

Generations of expert craftsmanship

Over 120 years ago, John Seamer left his employment as an estate carpenter at Waresley Park, Sandy, Bedfordshire and came to Derby, the home town of his wife to begin work on his own as a master carpenter.

Using traditional hand tools he built up the family carpentry and joinery business, J Seamer & Son, that has been carried on now by five generations of Seamers.

Seamers built several of the showcases which contain valuable pottery and silver in Derby's Council House. They also rebuilt much of the furniture at Kedleston Hall and relaid a floor at the Hall using oak that had been felled on the estate.

By 1975, the company's centenary, the original John Seamer's great grandson, Frank, was at the helm. This important milestone was celebrated with a formal dinner and ball for customers, suppliers and senior staff which was attended by the mayor and mayoress of Derby at the time, Councillor and Mrs George Salt.

Careful craftsmanship and a good reputation sell themselves and progress has been steady and pleasing for the company. However their history has not been free from incident, particularly during the eighties. In May 1981 an armed man being sought by the police for robbery from the Strutt Arms took refuge in the yard adjoining the Seamer premises, then in Woods Lane, off Abbey Street Armed police

in bullet-proof jackets surrounded them until the man surrendered.

In 1983 there was a serious fire which turned out to Seamers' advantage if to no-one else's. The Old Hall at Westwood Hall High School, a grade 2 listed, Victorian building was gutted. This was a situation where Seamers could come into their own. They were awarded a £40,000 contract to restore all the damaged woodwork in English oak.

Top: An early family picture with from left, Lawrence Seamer, William John Seamer, Gail Seamer and Frank Seamer. Left: The purpose-built workshop covering 6,500 sq.ft.

restoration was completed on time in September 1984.

A large amount of the company's work is centred on shopfitting but the firm's products were a little unusual in a world of mass-produced goods because many of the items they made for shop fittings were still largely produced by hand.

No detailed drawings of the Hall existed but Mr David Slade, the architect in charge was able to work from photographs of the Hall's panelling and moulding taken by sixth formers as part of a school project.

Seamers' contract included 120 square metres of dado and similar panelling, six pairs of panelled and moulded doors and frames, very elaborate front entrance doors, folding shutters to bay windows and the magnificent dog-leg staircase. The

However, Seamers did, of course obtain sophisticated machinery when it became available and use it when the job requires it. Current Seamer technology includes a spindle moulder, four cutters, a mortiser and a tenoner for joints, a ripsaw and a sanding machine to name but some.

Recent markets have included building societies, the bingo and amusement industry and private customers. The company has risen to many unusual challenges including building suspended ceilings, security screens and bullet-proof doors, a sad reflection of the times we now live in. It is good to know, if we do have need of them that Seamers can supply them, aided by a loyal workforce, many of whom have practised their craft and skill with the company for more than a quarter of a century.

Above: Frank Seamer, great grandson of the founder. *Above left:* A beautiful carved staircase in the Old Hall at Westwood Hall High School. *Left:* The Woods Lane premises. *Below:* An exterior view of the modern premises at Shaftesbury Street South.

Supplying the needs of local offices

The clatter of printing presses and the exciting smell of ink and new paper; this was the atmosphere, back in the mid-nineteenth Century, that provided the training ground for the keen young apprentice James Harwood at Benham's, the Colchester publisher and printer. From this print room background the young man with printing ink in his blood arrived in Derby in 1864 and took up employment with Bemrose and Sons, a local firm of printers who had been established since 1827. He was just 23 years old.

He spent six years with Bemrose and Sons, developing and consolidating his skills. Then around 1870 - or possibly slightly earlier than that date - he was ready to move on. The enterprising young man bought an already established book-sellers and stationery business from one Peter Peal, situated in the Corn Market, Derby. In turn, the success of that business led him on to take over the premises of T Moult, a tailor, at No 8 Corn Market, and it was here that James Harwood was able to bring his personal talents and creativity to the fore, designing, printing, publishing and marketing his products.

A range of Christmas cards were among James Harwood's first creations, and these he printed - and successfully marketed - using his own designs. It is the 'Derby Almanac and Diary,' however, for which he was particularly remembered. Mr Harwood compiled and edited the publication from the date it first appeared in 1873 until his death in 1925, when the Almanac was in its 53rd year. In 1879 he initiated 'Harwood's ABC Railway Guide,' followed in July 1893 by a weekly magazine, 'The Derby Comet.' Retail sales continued from the Corn Market site. As his business continued to expand it became necessary to open further premises, and by 1885 a works and warehouse in Tenant Street was handling all wholesale orders. Within six years number 17 Tenant Street was being quoted as the sole business address - 'specially erected to our requirements.' By now James Harwood was a highly successful manufacturing stationer as well as selling commercial stationery and

business equipment.

In 1909, purpose built premises that incorporated a new warehouse, factory and shop were opened in Derwent Street.

James Harwood's personal interests went far wider than stationery, however. Over the years he built up a valuable collection of old china and books. He became a well-known public figure, bringing entertainment and culture to Derby. He leased the Corn Exchange as a theatre and brought the Carl Rosa Opera Co - and a number of celebrities, including the well-known and respected writer Charles Dickens - to perform there. Surprisingly, James Harwood was also responsible for establishing a skating rink on the Uttoxeter Road - and the first Turkish baths in Friar Gate, Derby. In turn-of-the-century USA, the craze for Turkish Bath parties swept New York.

After James Harwood died in 1926, the business became a private limited company, James Harwood Ltd, with his son John as the company's first Managing Director.

From the early years of the century up to the late 1950s the Harwood's range of books did well. Coal dealers' ledgers, bread and milk delivery books, rent books, bill heads, memo forms, and even cricket scoring books were best sellers and were sold by commercial stationers countrywide. Other stationery lines included self-inking stamp pads, marking inks, date stamps, printing outfits and type-cases.

As the pattern of retailing changed, however, a number of Harwoods' products went out of fashion. Moving with the times, the company developed the colour printing side of the business, publishing travel guides and holiday brochures. In 1964 the company decided to concentrate on office equipment and commercial stationery.

New showrooms in the city centre were acquired in the mid sixties and a further move was made quite recently to 30 Curzon Street, Derby. The company has developed into one of the Midlands leading distributors of office products with a number of large organisations, including local authorities and nationalised industries, among its customers. Today the company carries an enormous range of stationery, with more than 7,000 items and more than half a million envelopes on its stock list.

The company is still very much a family firm, numbering three of James Harwood's direct descendants among its major shareholders. The founder's tradition of supplying stationery and equipment to ensure the smooth running of a modern office has been continued to the present time, and will hopefully continue forward well into the next millennium.

Above: Queen Mary at Harwoods stand at the Royal Show on Osmaston Park, Derby in the mid 1930s.
Left: The premises at 30 Curzon Street, Derby.
Facing page, top: James Harwood.
Facing page, bottom: The composing room in Derwent Street, Derby in the mid 1950s.

Made with the best of everything

To have 'the nicest sweet shop in town', was Joseph William Thornton's aim when he decided to open his own shop in 1911. Could he have looked into the future, he would have been amazed and gratified to see the eventual overwhelming success of his first modest venture.

Joseph William had been a commercial traveller in sweets when he came to the decision to go into business on his own account, and he opened his first shop, 'The Chocolate Kabin', in Norfolk Street, Sheffield. Unfortunately, Joseph William died in 1919, at a relatively young age, leaving his two sons Norman and Stanley to carry on the business. The two brothers were determined to pursue the tradition of quality which Joseph William had set and that quality should always be linked to the Thorntons name.

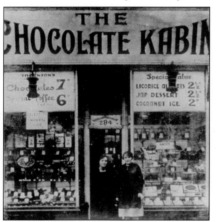

The two brothers worked hard and the business began to expand. By 1924 four shops were operating. One memorable Easter, the traditional Easter eggs were suffering a slow turnover, simply sitting on the shelves. Stanley and Norman Thornton, making their very first eggs, came up with the idea of personalising Easter eggs, writing the customer's name on the egg while they waited. The idea was a resounding success, and the

eggs were sold in neat white boxes for the very reasonable sum of 4d each.

Whilst Norman Thornton had a bent for marketing and retail it was his younger brother Stanley who enjoyed experimenting with recipes. Thus the company began to manufacture and retail its own products from its early beginnings. The real break-through came when Stanley Thornton, in 1925, came up with a new and delicious recipe - "made with the best of everything" - what he called simply "Special Toffee". Before very long, Special Toffee was accounting for half the firm's sales. Then and now it is the company's policy to use only the best raw materials, including sugar, milk, cream and dairy butter.

The success of the company was assured, and more shops were opened, at that time mainly in Yorkshire and Lancashire. By 1939 the company had around 30 shops, including the first Derby shop at 12 Market Place, and just before the outbreak of World War II the first purpose-built factory was opened in Sheffield. An amazing variety of sweets was produced: children could delight in the range of chocolate animals which included camels, dogs, lions, lambs, cows and turkeys, while their discerning parents could opt for butterscotch drops, rum and butters, marzipan, old fashioned treacle toffee and grapefruit caramels, to name only a few. By 1950 Derby had two more shops, one in St. James Street and their third one at 25 London Road, although this shop had closed by

Thornton's

1-lb. BOX

BRAZIL TOFFEE

4/1

PER BOX

Colours and flavours were mixed in by hand before the sweets were moulded from the sugar mass and twist wrapped.

The methods might have changed - but the old tradition is still there. Special Toffee is made from Stanley Thornton's original recipe and poured into special trays. The toffee is now automatically broken in the factory into bite sized pieces before being freshly delivered on a weekly basis to each of the company's retail shops.

1960. A new Thorntons outlet opened at 23 Theatre Walk, Derby in late 1975 and today there is a new shop in the Cornmarket and one in the Eagle Centre.

In 1954 a young Swiss Confisseur added his skills to those of the Thornton family, adapting Swiss recipes to produce a whole new range of chocolates. Today, Thorntons Continental Chocolates is the UK's biggest range of specialist chocolate assortments.

Derbyshire is now Thorntons sole centre for manufacturing and distribution, the original Sheffield factory having been closed in the mid 1980s. Special Toffee and sugar confectionery continue to be produced at the Belper factory, which was opened in 1946. All the company's chocolates are manufactured at Thornton Park near Alfreton, a site which was opened by Her Majesty the Queen in March 1985.

Whilst many of Thorntons products continue to be hand finished modern technology has been introduced wherever possible. Michael Thornton still remembers the days of his apprenticeship when he learnt the business from scratch. In those days, the 1950s, for boiled sweets the sugar mixture was cooked on large gas stoves in copper pans and hand poured onto water cooled steel slabs.

Thorntons is still very much a family firm. Michael Thornton is today the firm's deputy chairman, and his cousin John is chairman. It is the cousins' hope that another generation of Thorntons will continue to be involved in the running of the company.

The 1990s saw Thorntons sales top £100 million, with a total of over 500 shops throughout the United Kingdom and the Republic of Ireland. Each one continues to have the same aim as their founder, Joseph William - to be the nicest sweet shop in town.

Above: The Queen officially opened Thornton Park in March 1985. *Below: A modern Thorntons shop.* ***Facing***

From a back garden hobby to a UK leader

Quarndon Electronics was founded in 1962 by J.D.L. (David) Rose, a qualified Chartered Accountant, who had served two years in the RAF, returning to his Accountancy firm in 1961.

The company was originally formed so that he could obtain a wide range of parts at wholesale prices rather than relying on a retailer in Derby. The first premises were a converted stable at the family home in Quarndon. These premises were ideal for the first 18 months while QE was a hobby - making audio equipment for various people and some industrial equipment for local businesses.

In 1963 the firm of Chartered Accountants offered David a partnership which was of course interesting. They then ruined the discussion as it drew to a close by saying "you will have to pack in that electronics nonsense!" This was so annoying to David that he immediately declined their offer and gave them his notice.

There was further industrial work concerned with beer bottle labelling machines, coal mine signalling and temperature control. This required larger premises in Slack Lane situated over the Wine and Spirit department of Burrows & Sturgess Ltd with access by an exterior iron staircase. Reps and customers had to be directed to go up the iron staircase.

The mining system required the new range of silicon transistors that had been introduced by Texas Instruments. As these were on 26 weeks delivery he decided to buy extra quantities which also enabled him to obtain better pricing. This led to the idea of offering these items for sale. The first advert of 1/8th page in Wireless World produced 380 replies and £90 sales in the first month - doubling thereafter month by month.

Following this introduction into distribution as the first distributor for Texas Instruments in the UK, the company took on more of their products as they introduced them. Additionally they were approached by other new semiconductor firms wanting to market their products.

Good business relations with practically all the U.K.s Universities and Colleges along with many research and development departments of all types of firms who had bought various parts from the company but who were extremely interested in the Texas 74 Logic Family. This family and upgraded versions were used extensively to make all types of industrial equipment. QE's booklets which were prepared in-house gave concise data on the range

available proved very popular, so much so that Texas asked the company to reprint it for them for use in Scandinavia.

By 1970 premises were built to accommodate the expanding business on the site still occupied today. The first microprocessors appeared in the mid 1970s and with the extensive franchises at that time they developed a universal microcomputer system. This system could accommodate six boards; the front one was always the CPU card and versions were available for 8080, 8085, 2650, 6800, Z80, 8086 and Z8000. A variety of memory and interface cards could be used in the five remaining slots - the important factor being that they were used with all the CPU cards. This made an extremely attractive package for Universities who bought one system to cover all the processors available at that time rather than several systems from various manufacturers all operating in a different manner.

The company's activity in selling components by mailing technical details contrasted with distributors appointed later who provided little or no technical expertise but had reps carrying out a commodity sales operation.

In the early 1990s a major change took place. Most of the manufacturers decided to have distributors who covered Europe offering the franchise to American distributors who had set up or bought existing distributors in each country. So after 30 years working with Texas Instruments the QE's direct relationship finished. The company does retain strong links with Texas and Philips who particularly appreciate their work with micro-controllers and video graphics parts thereby enabling them to continue to promote and supply their products. One advantage of this less formal arrangement (the franchise agreement restricted the company's ability to buy from other suppliers), is that QE has now built-up contacts world-wide and can in fact offer a far greater range of product now than the company could do previously. Presenting and marketing this range is the company's challenge for the future.

Above: The custom built premises on Slack Lane.
Left: The popular manuals.
Facing page, top left: David Rose, whose hobby began the business.
Facing page, bottom: Jack Billinge, who made all kinds of equipment that was not available on the market. (Inset) A tape reader produced by QE in 1972.

Cultivating Agriculture

Acres (Willington) Ltd was established in 1947. Its founders were a business management graduate Frank Fryer, an engineer Fred Clayton and an agricultural engineer Roger Collins. The company repaired and maintained agricultural machinery from premises on Twyford road which was originally a farm building.

Acres' very first product, the Rotary Cultivator won a gold medal at the 1949 Three counties Show in Worcester and was exported through out the world right up to a shipment to Australia in 1965. Roger Collins later left the company, after which its emphasis was on horticultural engineering. Goods made were sold through Lawrence Edwards & Company Ltd. In 1962, at the Chelsea Flower Show, the first Soil Steriliser was exhibited. Two years later Acres improved on this with a steriliser using a cascading principle which is still in use today.

By 1969, Frank Fryer, the remaining director, was joined by John Large. By then the firm was supplying keg trucks to brewers and trolleys to Rolls Royce and Pirelli.

By the mid 70s the product range had extended to include soil processing equipment and treadle - operated woodworking lathes which John Large had designed and manufactured before joining Acres. In 1974 when ill-health forced Frank Fryer to retire, Derek Vallis joined the firm as sales director. The horticultural range was developed to meet the changing needs of a growing leisure industry. Also, an electric, variable speed lathe was developed for use in schools, colleges and light industry.

Mr Vallis purchased Mr Large's share in the company when he retired in 1984. Under Mr Vallis's leadership the trading emphasis has changed. Now, machining and fabrication, undertaken on a sub-contract basis is an equal part of the firm's business to manufacturing its own product range. Mr Vallis believes the company will probably form two divisions.

The existing staff form a solid foundation for growth. Their ability and enthusiasm to maintain the company's reputation, product range and success, ensure it is well placed for entry into the next millenium.

Above: The Derbyshire Show in 1950. Acres stand.
Below: Built on a Rolls-Royce chassis, Acres flagship their first delivery vehicle.

The company that has passed the test of time

The history of Coe's (Derby) Ltd dates back to before 1950 and to a garden shed behind the family home of Bernard Harrison where a spray packaging process was developed. When, in 1951, this 'development' became too much for the neighbours, the company 'Bernard Johns' was formed and sited in a lock-up garage in the centre of Derby. Initially this infant company provided sprayed, flexible, plastic blanking covers and high frequency weld sealing of plastic products for such as Rolls Royce.

Bernard Harrison had joined Rolls Royce after a brief period as a chemist, becoming a leading engineer during the war, and finally oversaw the packaging of engines for worldwide dispatch. He was well placed the venture out on his own and begin a company which worked along those lines. By 1956 the firm commenced fabrication of items in glass fibre laminates. This was a relatively new process and since skilled laminators were none existent the company had to train from scratch. About the same time the firm opened a shop in Derby town centre called The Plastic Centre which sold anything in plastic.

In 1957 the company had grown to such an extent that, having already moved from the lock-up to an old flourmill, it was forced to build its own factory at Ascot Drive.

The move coincided with a change of name to Coe's of Derby.

It was at this point that Bernard Harrison invented a tool control system that is still being manufactured today. One of the earlier boxes was supplied to the old aircraft carrier the Ark Royal, having passed all the MoD tests. "Not passed my test yet" said the Captain and threw the box from the flight deck onto the concrete dockside below, where it was retrieved in perfect condition. Since then it has received great praise and has proved to be a valuable asset to the armed forces

and police, so much so, that in 1970 Bernard Harrison was awarded the MBE for services to the Crown. Coe's remains a family business and continues its close links with Rolls Royce and the MoD but now produces a diverse range of high quality glass reinforced plastic products for almost any application. With its own design facilities, Coe's can supply affordable answers to any clients' GRP requirements and is now a countrywide leader in its field.

Above: From 1957, testing the first box.
Top: An early letterhead.
Left: The Ark Royal Toolbox that passed 'all the tests'.

Towards two centuries of service

Eggleston Bros Limited is one the oldest established companies in Derby dating back to 1809. The original company was founded as Joseph E Hunt, Ironmongers in St Peter's Street where today Marks & Spencer is situated. Matthias Eggleston, a confectioner of Iron Gate, Derby, bought the Iron Bar Warehouse part of the business at 40 London Road for two of his four sons, Walter and George. In 1902 Walter and George moved to 3 Derwent Street next door to the Royal Standard Public House.

The business partnership was dissolved in 1914 and Walter continued on his own. A few years later he took over the business of John Beatson & Son, Railway Engineers. For a number of years the two firms were run separately, but were amalgamated in 1932 to trade under the name of Eggleston Bros & Beatson, a name still remembered today by the older generation. This new business concentrated wholly on Iron and Steel merchanting.

Over the years many changes took place in their trade and in the early part of this century the main stock consisted of wrought iron, but this gave way to mild and alloy steels, black and bright which were eventually requested for 99% of the work for which iron had been used.

Two World Wars provided Eggleston's with work which enabled them to survive during periods of difficulty for the majority of businesses.

The Second War brought licencing, pricing and rationing. The post war years then produced confusing legislation including nationalisation, denationalisation and re-nationalisation and then the rationalisation of the steel industry and it's products, which brought about an amazing growth of the market share for stockholders.

The Derwent Street premises had space restrictions and the steel bars were often stood on end. It seemed a good idea at the time as nobody had heard of the domino effect. There was quite a crash when the bar stock collapsed taking with it a part of the building. Miraculously nobody was hurt. In 1950 Walter Eggleston died aged 82 and having no immediate family the business

*Above: An early invoice. Left: The Confectioners shop which was established in 1820. **Facing page top:** The Eggleston brothers and friends in the late 1800's. On the left is Walter, second on the back row is George, centre is Albert John (Mayor of Derby 1919/20) and on the right is Cantrell. **Facing page bottom:** Two of today's director's inspecting the damage in the late 1940s.*

passed to his nephew Joseph Eggleston Burrows, known as Seph, who was the last person in the business to bear the name Eggleston.

It became obvious that the premises were too small and as the backing in of vehicles brought traffic chaos to Derwent Street which was the main route to Nottingham and Mansfield, a new site would have to be found. In 1964 Seph Burrows sold the old premises to Kennings and moved to Stuart Street, at the same time changing the firm's name to Eggleston Bros. Limited. As a result of this move into a larger warehouse it became possible to improve the delivery service and customers who wished to collect their materials had ample off road parking space.

Two loading bays were covered by gantry cranes to give a quick turnaround. The range of materials and sizes stocked was comprehensive in both ferrous and non-ferrous products. For the next eight years space was not a problem until the Derby Inner Ring Road was built taking valuable land from the Company.

In 1977 Seph Burrows died at the age of 77, still in harness and another member of the family, Tony Hewitt took over, whose share of the firms history has included a steel strike and two trade recessions. During the last major recession in 1990, sales figures plummeted and the performance graph on the wall was taken down to avoid depressing the onlookers. Fortunately the following years brought an improvement in demand for steel products and the company was again able to expand.

A relatively small firm in a very large competitive market, the company with a staff of 23 is still stocking, processing and supplying a wide range of mild steels and non-ferrous metals to industrial customers all over the East Midlands. In 1996 they were awarded the prestigious BS EN ISO 9002 Certification which brought with it International as well as European-wide recognition for quality. As Managing Director Tony Hewitt remarked the award was "a sure sign that we can compete in todays market place".

Today and hopefully in the future the company is holding it's own surviving many battles by matching the big boys with the use of the latest computer technology and modern equipment. The management are proud of the firm's history and even more proud of the staff who are all aware of the David versus Goliath conflict - the family business surviving against the giants.

Eggleston Bros. is looking forward to completing it's second century of service early in the New Millennium.

Facing page top: J.E. Burrows (Seph), who served the Company for forty nine years, twenty seven of them as a proprietor.

Facing page bottom: Different modes of transportation in the 1960's.

Far right: A section of the Company's processing facility.

Right: A small section of the flat stock.

Below right: The Company fleet.

Below: Tony Hewitt (centre) with John Canning (fourth left), of Premier Assessments presenting the Certificate of Accreditation of ISO 9002 to Richard Hewitt (fourth right), the Director responsible for Quality Assurance, together with some members of the staff.

The firm with its clients in mind

Shevill Parkes was founded in 1966 by a partnership of three men, Peter Parkes, Harry Bodkin and Dick Birch. Working out of offices in Gower Street, Derby

The infant company soon established itself as a leading broker in the construction, civil engineering and plant hire industry. The firm remained at Gower Street for three years until the move to Charnwood Street.

There were the usual problems with a new business, compounded by the fact that the men were very young. Dick Birch was just 24. Inexperience and naivety had to be overcome and the men soon learned that to give too much credit was not always a good idea.

Dick Birch acquired control of the company in 1970. He was well placed to run the business as he had a insurance history of over a decade, working with Royal Insurance in the early 1960s and moving to Barnes & Co Insurance Brokers in 1964.

The firm has grown quietly but confidently over the years, with Dick Birch taking on a partner, Mick Dunn. Mick joined as a director and share-holder.

In 1995 the company was able to purchase another Derby insurance broker, Ryan Benson.

For a small company, Shevill Parkes has a large number of academically qualified directors and staff who pride themselves on their ability to act

The mid 1990s saw the arrival of Derek Parrett to develop new business, especially within the professions and manufacturing industry. Then, more recently, Roger Missin was appointed to Financial Services as a specialist in corporate financial planning.

Over the years the company has established a reputation for quality, integrity and professionalism. The byword is service.

Diversification took place in the mid 1990s with the birth of Shevill Parkes Financial Services Limited, a completely separate company offering independent advice and specialising in corporate and personal financial planning.

in their clients' best interests at all times. Their clients are generally small to medium sized businesses, who

are mainly based in the East Midlands. They encompass all sections of the professions, commerce and industry, from football clubs to motorcycle manufacturers. The company's packages are tailored for the needs of both small and large companies, minimising costs and disruption to the business.

From modest beginnings the company has grown, by sheer hard work and foresight. Now as we approach the millennium, thoughts inevitably turn to the future. Shevill Parkes offers sound advice and a quality service that is unrivalled in its field.

Above: The main office staff.
Below left: The Administration staff.
Below right: A newsletter issued to clients.
Facing Page: The Directors of the company.

Williams PLC - Protecting people and property from fire and intrusion throughout the world

Williams PLC today is a leading international security group. Its business is protecting people and property from fire and intrusion throughout the world.

Through leading brand names in global fire and security, such as Yale, Kidde and Chubb, Williams supplies to industrial and commercial, aerospace and defence and residential markets. Its products and services are unrivalled in the worldwide market for range, quality and reliability. These products range from CCTV, electronic access control and remote monitoring, to industrial fire detection and suppression systems and security hardware such as locks, high security safes and exit devices. The group employs over 38,000 people worldwide and has manufacturing, sales and service operations in over 35 countries.

Above: Williams PLC's Chairman Sir Nigel Rudd, left, and Chief Executive Roger Carr. Left: Safety control of a technical product for the aerospace industry. The product has undergone research and development for protection from fire.

Williams' origins were as a tiny Welsh engineering company established in Caerphilly in 1957. By February 1982 W. Williams & Sons had run into severe financial difficulties. It was then that it began a new life when it was acquired by two ambitious young accountants, Nigel Rudd, who was born and bred in Derby, and Brian McGowan.

Williams Holdings made its first appearance on the Derby landscape just nine months later with the acquisition of Ley's Foundries and Engineering; based in Colombo Street next to the old Baseball Ground. Ley's, comprised Beeston Boilers, Ewart Chainbelt and Ley's Malleable Castings. It was one of Europe's largest malleable iron foundries, but had fallen on hard times as a result of the decline in the

British motor car industry. The company was losing money, but provided a crucial platform from which to grow the new Williams group. Roger Carr, who worked at Ley's, was to become instrumental in building the Williams group in the future, first as head of the "special

Above: Ley's Works on Colombo Street, pictured in the 1950s, where Williams began its association with Derby in 1982.
Right: Williams PLC's head office today, in Sir Frank Whittle Road, Derby.

operations" team which was responsible for turning round acquired companies, and then later as Chief Executive.

From its humble beginnings, Williams soon became one of the "stock market darlings" of the eighties, achieving rapid growth through its strategy of acquiring underperforming and undermanaged companies and turning them around.

By the late eighties Williams' ambitions had changed - it had altered its focus in order to build a business of lasting quality and excellence. In order to achieve this, the company began to buy branded, market leading businesses, manufacturing building products and fire protection and security products.

In the nineties the group became a member of Britain's top 100 publicly quoted companies with sales of over £2 billion. Williams has also won Industry Week's 100 Best Managed Companies award for the last two years.

Above and Below: Early Chubb deliveries destined for distribution around the Commonwealth.

Significant milestones along the way have been the acquisitions of Pilgrim House in 1988, which moved the group into fire protection with Kidde International; and Yale and Valor in 1991, which took the group into security products. During the nineties the group continued to strengthen its presence in these markets through an ongoing programme of in-fill acquisitions and organic growth.

The mid-nineties saw Williams sharpen its business focus even further. The group began a phased withdrawal from its building products businesses to concentrate purely on building a global fire and security company. In June 1996, Williams sold its electronics business to a management buyout team. Later in the year, its UK building products businesses (including brands such as Aqualisa, Valor, Rawlplug and

This picture: Williams' companies produce highly sensitive equipment to detect and suppress fires and explosions in a wide range of situations from boiler safety in schools and hospitals, to major chemical processing plants and offshore rigs.

Smallbone) were also sold to a management team. The European fillers and coatings companies were sold to ICI in 1998.

During the past two years, principal acquisitions have been Sicli, the leading fire protection company in France; Sides, the leading fire and rescue vehicle manufacturer in France; and Tesa, the market leader in security products in Spain and number two in the world market for electronic hotel locks.

Undoubtedly Williams' most significant acquisition in its history to date, was that of Chubb in February 1997. This acquisition established Williams on the world map as a global leader in fire protection and security, and took Williams into new markets with its Yale, Kidde and Chubb brands. Chubb took Williams into higher growth areas such as CCTV, remote monitoring and electronic access control. It also dramatically increased the company's involvement in service related businesses, such as central monitoring and security personnel, which provide recurring sources of revenue for the company.

Above: The Security Monitoring Centres rely on an experienced team of security professionals to respond to alarms and emergencies quickly and effectively 24 hours a day. *Below:* Improved security from Yale, serving residential and commercial customers world-wide.

Following the Chubb acquisition and as a reflection of the sharpened focus of the group,

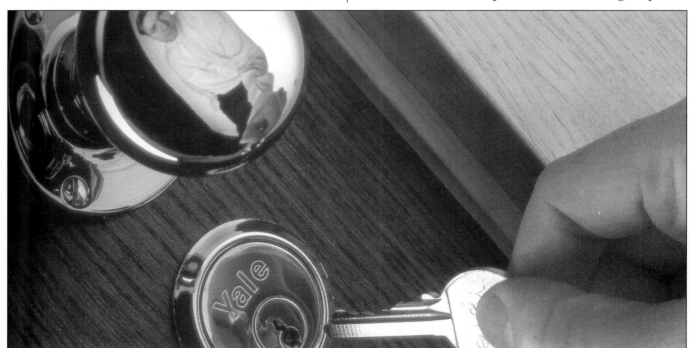

Williams Holdings changed its name to Williams PLC in 1997. Williams PLC provides sophisticated monitoring systems for fire and intruder detection for all environments. For example you can expect to see Chubb CCTV cameras monitoring locations ranging from hospitals to shopping centres and football stadiums. As well as providing the systems, Williams offers security personnel services for crowd control, guarding, patrol services and even armed response.

All fire protection systems, portable extinguishers and alarm systems are checked regularly by service engineers, to ensure they are always ready to be used in the event of any emergency.

Williams fire protection products use the latest technology and are supplied to industrial and commercial, and aerospace and defence markets. For example, Williams provides high sensitivity smoke detectors which use laser based technology, and optical flame sensors with the ability to distinguish false alarms from real ones.

In addition, Williams offers a wide range of residential products including fire extinguishers and carbon monoxide detectors. In fact, Williams is one of the world's largest manufacturers of portable fire extinguishers for the home.

Williams' security hardware is also well known throughout the world through various branded products. All have excellent reputations for quality and reliability whether a Yale padlock, a Union mortice lock or a Chubb safe.

Williams and the Community

Williams is dedicated to supporting young people in the development of their talents, and has continued to support programmes committed to the development and training of young people in music, sport and education.

The group continues to be an active sponsor of music with a long-standing commitment to the National Youth Orchestra, one of the world's finest youth orchestras. This year, Williams showed its cultural commitment by saving Derbyshire's Buxton Festival from potential collapse with a vital eleventh-hour injection of cash.

In the area of sport, the group has maintained its level of sponsorship, particularly in Derby, with lawn tennis, cricket and soccer benefiting from this active support.

In education, Williams has maintained its commitment to Derby Boys' Grammar School and Landau Forte City Technology College. Recently, the group has contributed to the Prince's Youth Business Trust to support entrepreneurial flair and assist in the development of small businesses.

The charitable donation policy of Williams has been to focus resources on organisations that are dedicated to helping sick or disadvantaged children. Beneficiaries include the Royal School for deaf children, the Rainbow Hospice at Loughborough and various other local charities.

Left: *Williams supports the National Youth Orchestra to benefit the community as a whole.*

The lower part of St Peter's Street, dating from the 1950s

ACKNOWLEDGMENTS

TONY BOWLER, DERBY HISTORIAN AND NEWSPAPER COLUMNIST

DERBY LOCAL STUDIES LIBRARY

DERBY MUSEUM

ROYAL CROWN DERBY PORCELAIN MUSEUM

W.W WINTERS LIMITED

MANY OF THE PHOTOGRAPHS IN THIS BOOK ARE FROM W.W WINTERS LIMITED.
PRINTS OF THESE PHOTOGRAPHS CAN BE ORDERED BY TELEPHONING 01332 345224